WALKING
ITALY

*For all the walkers, would-be walkers, armchair travellers and daytime dreamers.
And for Glenys, with love*

What people say about *Walking Italy*

'Whether you are as enamored of the pleasures of hiking or walking as the author has been over her lifetime, or an armchair traveller or Italy dreamer wishing for a thrilling read, you might, like me, fall helplessly and gratefully into the fascinating and evocative pages of this deeply knowledgeable guide... Besides the delicious prose and historical perspectives in "Walking Italy," there are useful maps, links, practical suggestions, and resources for travelers who prefer slow, intimate travel to being hustled on guided packaged tours along the well-traveled tourist paths of Venice-Florence-Rome-home.'   **Julia della Croce, award-winning writer and author**

'As well as instructions for walks, Rachael also gives a detailed history of each area... I have a huge library of books about Italy and this brilliant book is going to be joining them on my shelves. If you love walking amidst beautiful scenery with the added bonus of good food along the way, this is certainly the book for you.'   **Jane Keightley, travel writer and Italy specialist**

'Two things stand out to me in this excellent, thoughtfully written guidebook: Rachael's indepth, practical knowledge of Italy and its places, cuisine and traditions, and – as importantly – her deep love for the country and its history, traditions and landscapes. Whether you're planning your next adventure of simply appreciating the beautiful photos and vivid descriptions of 'Il Bel Paese', *Walking Italy* is sure to inspire more than a wee bit of wanderlust.'   **Elizabeth Heath, Italy travel writer and owner of Villaggio Tours, Umbria**

'Admire the beauty of Tuscany, Umbria or Lake Como from a different perspective, with curiosity, respect for nature and a little sense of adventure.'   **Monica Neroni, Lake Como Tourist Guide**

'Clearly put together with love and passion for walking and Italy. ... The writing is entertaining, the photographs are stunning; a perfect book even just for armchair travellers who just want to learn about Italy while putting their feet up.'   **Kate Orson, travel journalist**

'A Yorkshire lass, hiking is in Rachael's DNA, and having lived in Italy for more than 25 years, this captivating country of a myriad of geographical contrasts is now her stomping ground. *Walking Italy* is a collection of favourite walks, pilgrims' routes and ancient tracks, each with a fascinating story to tell... Keep this handy, intelligent guide tucked in your rucksack (virtual or real) to step into the shoes of pilgrims and travellers down through the centuries and experience your own modern-day adventure.'   **Amanda Robinson, Editor, *Italia!* Magazine, www.italytravelandlife.com**

'A wonderful careful work; a timely and practical treasure-trove guide for lovers of walking, Italy and eating.'   **Rachel Roddy, writer and author**

'Martin's enthusiasm and knowledge shine through, as does her personal connection to the places she writes about. Blending historical background, cultural insight, and up-to-date practical advice suitable for walkers of all experience levels, this travel guide is an indispensable companion for those who want to soak up the best of Italy's landscapes and culture at their own pace.'   **Claire Speak, Editor, The Local Italy**

WALKING
ITALY

A Guide for Tourists and Armchair Travellers

RACHAEL MARTIN

WHITE OWL

AN IMPRINT OF PEN & SWORD BOOKS LTD.
YORKSHIRE – PHILADELPHIA

First published in Great Britain in 2024 by
White Owl
An imprint of
Pen & Sword Books Ltd.
Yorkshire - Philadelphia

Copyright © Rachael Martin, 2024

ISBN 978 1 39903 134 9

The right of Rachael Martin to be identified as author of
this work has been asserted by her in accordance with the
Copyright, Designs and Patents Act 1988.

A CIP catalogue record for this book is available from the
British Library.

Printed and bound in India by Replika Press Pvt. Ltd.
Design: SJmagic DESIGN SERVICES, India.

Pen & Sword Books Ltd. incorporates the imprints of Pen &
Sword Books: After the Battle, Archaeology, Atlas, Aviation,
Battleground, Discovery, Family History, History, Maritime,
Military, Politics, Select, Transport, True Crime, Fiction, Frontline
Books, Leo Cooper, Praetorian Press, Seaforth Publishing,
Wharncliffe and White Owl.

For a complete list of Pen & Sword titles please contact

PEN & SWORD BOOKS LIMITED
George House, Beevor Street, Off Pontefract Road, Hoyle
Mill, Barnsley, South Yorkshire, England, S71 1HN.
E-mail: enquiries@pen-and-sword.co.uk
Website: www.pen-and-sword.co.uk

or

PEN AND SWORD BOOKS
1950 Lawrence Rd, Havertown, PA 19083, USA
E-mail: uspen-and-sword@casematepublishers.com
website: www.penandswordbooks.com

MIX
Paper | Supporting
responsible forestry
FSC
www.fsc.org
FSC™ C016779

Walking along Lake Como. Rachael Martin

boumenjapet / Adobe Stock

Andrea Vismara / Adobe Stock

CONTENTS

FOREWORD

Italy has always held an irresistible allure, with its rich tapestry of history, culture, and breathtaking landscapes. As a long-time resident of this incredible country, I have spent over thirty years exploring its hidden gems and well-trodden paths alike. When I first delved into this book, I was struck by the comprehensive nature of her work, and her passion that shines through every page. Rachael has crafted more than just a travel guide; she has provided a window into the soul of Italy.

This book is a treasure trove of suggestions on where to walk and the best times of year to embark on these adventures. But it goes beyond that, offering practical advice on what to wear, where to eat, what to visit and where to stay. Her attention to detail ensures that every traveller, whether on foot or from the comfort of their armchair, can fully immerse themselves in the Italian experience. As someone who loves, and highly recommends, travelling during the Slower Season Months, I particularly appreciate Rachael's emphasis on exploring Italy at this time. Her choices reflect a deep understanding of how to make the most of each destination, revealing both the famous landmarks and the hidden corners that many visitors overlook. It's clear that she has walked these paths herself, soaking in the true essence of each locale.

One of the most delightful aspects of this book is how Rachael introduces us to Italy 360°, offering a holistic view that includes not only the sights but also the history, local customs and culinary delights. Her recommendations on where to eat and what to drink are invaluable, ensuring that readers can savour the authentic flavours of Italy as they travel. From the majestic peaks of the Aosta Valley to the historic wonders beyond Rome, and from the serene shores of Lake Como, which I proudly call my backyard, to the vibrant fields of Castelluccio in Umbria, Rachael's vivid descriptions bring each location to life. Her enthusiasm is contagious, inspiring readers to lace up their walking shoes and discover these beautiful places for themselves.

Reading this book I am reminded of the countless adventures I have shared with my husband Alessandro and our three Labradors Lola, Bella and Frida. Each journey one enjoys in Italy is always enriched by the people you meet along the way, and Rachael captures this beautifully. She truly shows us that travelling in Italy is not just about the destinations but also about the connections we make and the stories we gather. 'Walking Italy' is more than a guidebook; it is an invitation to experience Italy in all its glory. Whether you are planning your next trip or simply dreaming from your favourite reading nook, Rachael's book will transport you into the heart of this incredible country.

Enjoy the journey – ci vediamo in Italia!

Andrea Grisdale
Founder and CEO IC Bellagio

PREFACE

It's a Saturday in July and I'm standing at the bottom of a mountain with my newly acquired Italian boyfriend. We're about to go sleep in a tent up a mountain with some of his friends. I'm excited about going up the mountain because I love mountains. I'm less excited about carrying the rucksack he's holding out for me, particularly as it contains what appears to be at least a two-litre bottle of wine. I didn't carry the wine - love wasn't that blind or stupid. I was glad I didn't, especially as the route we were about to go up is known as Il Calvario (The Ordeal). It lived up to its name. I got up there to a place called Alpe Angeloga, and loved it. I'd never slept in a tent up a mountain before, but I knew that it was something I wanted to do again.

Fast forward twenty-five years and the boyfriend has become my husband and we have two boys to share our love of walking up mountains. They've come with us from an early age, their two sets of little legs carrying their own rucksacks.

They now send me photos from summits that would probably just give me vertigo. We often go off together as a family. I'm one of the locals who sets off in her car with her family along the SS 36 Lago di Como e dello Spluga (Lake Como and the Spluga Valley) towards Lecco, up along Lake Como with those fantastic views, and then off into the mountains beyond. We've recently spent entire summers up there to escape the heat but also to just enjoy the mountain life, its quiet rhythms and savour its light. This is where the idea for this book began to take shape one summer, when I was walking the Via Spluga.

As a girl, I'd go walking with my family in the Yorkshire Dales. I'd stride out ahead, making up stories as I went. Now I'm more likely to research the stories those places hold. I live in a village up on a hill, surrounded by mountains, with a valley known as La Valletta, or the little valley, which opens out before it. It's one of the places where I feel most at home,

Alpe Angeloga. Rachael Martin

amidst the allotments which remind me of my childhood and surrounded by the mountains of my life today. Monte Rosa stands in the distance on the border between the Aosta Valley and Piedmont, there in all her beauty. In spite of the fact she turns pink or rose in the light, *rosia* in Latin means glacier, and on Monte Rosa you will indeed find glaciers.

There is always a sense of adventure in going somewhere new, whether physically or via our imaginations from the comfort of our own homes. I hope you enjoy the adventures offered within these pages.

ACKNOWLEDGEMENTS

A big thank you to Jonathan Wright, Janet Brookes, Charlotte Mitchell and everyone at Pen & Sword Books. Thank you, as always, to Stefano, for his continued love and support. To Giovanni and Gabriele, who send me all the videos and photos from high-up places - keep aiming high. And to Rachel, for sharing the excitement and enthusiasm towards Italian places as I wrote.

INTRODUCTION

When William Wordsworth left Cambridge University in 1790, he went on a walking tour to France and Italy. He walked extensively in the Alps and then came to Lake Como, where he went walking above Gravedona and got lost. He sat on a rock until morning, and then wrote about it all in *The Prelude*. Wordsworth was part of the trend for foreign travel, which was first called the 'Grand Tour' by writer and priest Richard Lessels in his 1670 book *The Voyage of Italy*. Wealthy young men and aristocratic heirs set off to Europe. Italy was an essential stop, especially Rome, Florence, Venice and Naples, and art and culture a priority. If you were rich, you travelled by carriage, and were sometimes carried in a sedan over the Alps, as any route to Italy usually involved the Alps. Young men went home and told tales of their experiences, and writers went home and wrote about it. What this all meant was that Italy began to become known. Every time you visit Italy, you're following in a long tradition of those who have visited before you. You might

Andrea Vismara / Adobe Stock

stevanzz / Adobe Stock

not write poetry like Wordsworth, but you could still go off wandering above Lake Como, although the getting lost part is really not advisable!

This is a book about walking in Italy. I wrote it because I wanted to share with you some of the places you can enjoy simply by putting one foot in front of the other. You'll find merchants' ways, pilgrims' routes, Roman routes and other paths and tracks, all of which are testimonies to Italy's past. Some of the walks offer the chance to revisit much-loved places in a different way, such as the walks above Lake Como. Other walks may be new and introduce you to areas with which you might

not be familiar. The Via Francigena is one of the most famous pilgrimages in Europe, along with the Cammino de Santiago de Compostela. If you were to do the whole walk, you'd need to start in Canterbury and finish in Rome. That's around 2,000km, so I've focused on a couple of sections. One of these is up at the Colle del Gran San Bernardo (Great St Bernard's Pass) that links the Aosta Valley with Switzerland. Other walks are much shorter. In each case I look at the history, culture and places involved in each walk. I also give recommendations on where to stay and where to eat. When in Italy, eat the food and drink the wine. Speaking of wine, for wine-lovers there's a walk around the Chianti vineyards in Tuscany. What more could you want in life?

You don't have to be an expert walker to get something out of it. Think of this book as saying to you: this is what is here. You might choose to walk certain sections of a walk, or you may even plan to do the whole of a walk. That is your decision, and if you are planning to do a whole walk, then it's always a good idea to pace yourself. It's better to have an extra day in a destination and rest than find yourself overtired and wanting to give the whole thing up. Take it slow and steady and you'll get there eventually. Alternatively, you might choose to sit in the comfort of your own home with a nice glass of Italian red and a bowl of olives and dream of Italian climes.

Writing a book like this is as much about what to leave out as what to include. There is so much more I could have written about, other walks, regions and mountain ranges. Rather than include every region in Italy, I've focused on several. This is for practical reasons, as during a one or two-week holiday you might not want to go rushing off all over, but rather focus on walking in particular areas and fitting in some sightseeing at some stage. One way to do it is to alternate your days between sightseeing and walking, with the option of throwing a relax day in here and there. At one time I was the holiday maker who loved to go away and rush all over. Then I discovered a quieter, slower form of tourism, one in which focusing in on one area has proved to be infinitely rewarding. It gives you time to really get to know a place, enter deeper into its sense of place, the relationship its people have to it, and the effect it has on you.

With regards to walking equipment, this means a good pair of waterproof walking boots, waterproof jacket, fleece, a spare t-shirt in case you sweat while you're walking, drinking water and food. Believe me when I say that a decent pair of waterproof walking boots can make all the difference. I always wear those that come up to your ankles, as I find they give me better support. You might also want to consider getting one of those waterproof capes to protect your rucksack in case of downpours. One word about rucksacks; notice how it feels when you try it. If it offers good support, this will help save your back when you're out.

There is an unspoken rule when out walking. Everyone who is walking together stays together. The other rule is to know your limits, and to understand when it's time to turn back and protect the safety of all. We spend our lives hearing about how we should push ourselves out of our comfort zones. I personally don't recommend it. There's wisdom in staying in your comfort zone, especially when you're up in the mountains.

MAPS, FURTHER INFORMATION AND USEFUL LINKS

At the end of each section, you'll find links to maps and further information. Many walks have their own websites and sometimes accompanying apps with maps and often GPS references. You should always follow these when you are out on your walks. There are also various apps for mobile phones that transmit your GPS location should the need arise. The app 112 Where Are U lets you contact emergency services and automatically gives your GPS location. This is particularly worth considering if you're thinking of walking alone.

A WORD ABOUT MOUNTAINS

You can't write any book about walking in Italy without talking about its mountains. A mountain is classed as anything above 600m, which means that Italy is 35% mountains and 41% hills. This makes for a lot of mountains and hills. In the north of Italy there are the Alps, an arch-shaped mountain range that stretches for approximately 1,200km from Colle di Cadibona in Liguria to the Vrata mountain pass in Slovenia. From west to east, Italy borders France, Switzerland, Austria and Slovenia. The Appenines are often known as Italy's spine or backbone. They stretch from Liguria in the north-west, through

central Italy and down into the south and across to Sicily. The Appenines in Sicily are known as the Appeninno Siculo. These are lower and rounder mountains, without glaciers. The highest mountain in Sicily is a volcanò, Mount Etna, at 3,357m. Then there are the mountains in Sardinia, Italy's other main island, proving that Italy is as much about its mountains as its hilltop villages and cities of art.

SENTIERO ITALIA

The Sentiero Italia, or the Great Italian Trail, is a mountain trail which goes across the whole of Italy. At roughly 8,000km long, it's eight times the length of the Camino de Santiago, and one of the longest mountain trails in the world. The idea of a route to link all of Italy's mountain ranges was originally conceived by a group of hiking journalists in 1983. They formed the Sentiero Italia Hiking Association, which was then managed by the Italian Alpine Club. Later, the project fell into the background until in 2019, Yuri Basilicò, Sara Furlanetto and Giacomo Riccobono founded the Va' Sentiero project. Their goal was to travel the whole of the Sentiero Italia, map its ways and tell stories of the people and places they met along the way. From 2019 to 2021 they walked. They collected data and information which they then used for their Va' Sentiero website. This digital guide is accessible

Taiga / Adobe Stock

to anyone, with all the relevant maps, GPS, technical information, cultural notes, videos, photos and more. It provides a wealth of information. It's also a very enjoyable site to explore and learn more about Italy and its mountains.

The route begins in the Gulf of Trieste on the border with Slovenia, specifically at Albana, a hamlet belonging to Prepotto in the province of Udine.[1] From here it makes its way through each of Italy's twenty regions and sixteen of its national parks. The route involves a 35,000m elevation gain and 364 stages. It goes across the Alps from east to west, down along the Appenines to the south, where it then continues across to Sicily. From Sicily you then go to Sardinia, where the route ends in Orosei in the Gulf of Orosei, with a view of Corsica across the sea.[2] It's a route which celebrates and explores Italy's natural beauty, its places and the people and communities you meet. In 2022 Va' Sentiero was awarded the prestigious European Heritage Award for the category Citizens Engagement Awareness category.

In 2020 a joint project was set up by Club Alpino Italiano and the Ministry of the Environment for a new walk to be known as Sentiero dei Parchi, or Way of the Parks, which is based on Sentiero Italia. The walk follows a rough outline of the route the Sentiero Italia currently takes but is designed to take in all of Italy's national parks and UNESCO natural sites. There are currently five UNESCO natural sites in Italy. They include the pale mountains known as the Dolomites, with their incredible rock formations; Europe's highest active volcano Mount Etna; the Aeolian islands volcanic archipelago off Sicily; and the ancient primeval beech forests of the Carpathian Mountains. These forests are found in eighteen countries across Europe. In Italy, they go from Emilia-Romagna to Basilicata in the south. Monte San Giorgio, on the border with Switzerland, is the fifth UNESCO natural site. This pyramid-shaped mountain is considered the finest example of fossils from the Middle Triassic period when dinosaurs roamed the earth.

FURTHER INFORMATION

www.vasentiero.org is the digital guide produced by the project Va' Sentiero and is in both Italian and English. The book *Va' Sentiero: In Cammino per le Terre Alte d'Italia* by Juri Basilicò and Sara Furlanetto was published by Rizzoli in 2023. It's in Italian but if you have a basic working knowledge of written Italian, it's a great way to get to know the trail and mountains, and practice your Italian! The documentary *Alla Scoperta del Va' Sentiero* (discovering the Va' Sentiero) is also in Italian. It tells the story of the first seven months of the journey from its beginning in Friuli-Venezia Giulia to Marche.

You can also walk with the Va' Sentiero on their current expeditions along the trail. Over 3,000 people have already taken part. Details and dates can be found on their website.

THE VIA FRANCIGENA AND THE AOSTA VALLEY

→ Via Francigena – Canterbury to Rome
- Great St Bernard's Pass to Echevennoz

INTRODUCTION

The Valle D'Aosta, or Aosta Valley, is Italy's smallest region with its smallest population. It's a mountainous region of wild beauty and part of the Alps, the 1,200km long mountain range which stretches all along the north of Italy and forms a natural border between Italy and the rest of Europe. Italy has the largest percentage of Alps after Austria. Of a total of eighty-two peaks

Rachael Martin

lic00001 / Adobe Stock

reaching 4,000m or above, almost half of these are in Italy or have the Italian border running through them. The majority are in the Aosta Valley. In fact, the average altitude in the Aosta Valley is 2,100m, which makes it hardly surprising that it's sometimes known as the 'roof of Europe'. Mont Blanc, or Monte Bianco as the Italians call it, straddles the French-Italian border and at 4,809m is the highest mountain in the Alps and in Western Europe. Who has the summit is a contentious issue. The French say it's theirs, while the Italians say the border passes through it. If we go with the Italians,

this means that Italy's four highest peaks are all in the Aosta Valley: Monte Bianco, Monte Rosa (4,609m), Cervino/Matterhorn (4,478m) and Gran Paradiso (4,061m).

When you go to the Aosta Valley, what hits you is the height of these mountains. The Great St Bernard Pass goes through these mountains up at 2,469m. This is where Europe's oldest European Christian pilgrims' route, the Via Francigena, comes into Italy. The route is 2,000km long, and is also a historic trading and military route. Nowadays we drive through tunnels and over mountain passes, but in the past crossing the Alps was a difficult and sometimes dangerous journey. Most people walked. Others had mules or horses where this was possible, while if you were wealthy, you might be carried over in a sedan. It's a route which people have been crossing since Roman times and before. In 1846 Charles Dickens travelled over the Great St Bernard Pass by mule with his wife Kate and stayed the night at the Great Saint Bernard Hospice where the religious community there gave shelter to pilgrims and travellers. It was a pretty horrendous journey, and he must have been glad when it was over. Later, when he wrote *Little Dorrit*, he had the Dorrit family making the same journey.

It's easy enough to see Dickens' point, especially when you're up there and it's blowing a gale. Passing through mountains which reach 4,000m or above, or four-thousanders as they are sometimes known, isn't exactly a walk in the park. The weather conditions up at the mountain passes can be extreme and brutal. Moreover, they can change quickly. What starts out as a pleasant sunny day can turn into snow if the weather conditions are that way inclined. If you're planning to walk here, make sure you're well informed of the forecast and conditions before starting out. After all, we're up in what is known as *alta montagna*, high mountains above 1,500m, where winters are longer and summers are shorter. These types

of walks can also be more demanding, especially as you get higher up. Bear in mind the altitude, which if you're not used to it, can make walking more tiring. Spring and summer were popular seasons for making pilgrimages, but even in summer at that altitude the weather can change. It can also reach startlingly low temperatures, is notoriously windy, and is one of the last places you would particularly want to be on a dark, snowy night. When the wind gets up and the rain starts pouring, it reminds you of the power of nature. When the sun shines and there is a clear view of the mountains, it feels like the most beautiful place on earth. This is where Saint Bernard set up his hospice and where the Romans built a temple many years before. It's a mixture of faith and history, of place and the people who passed through it, and this is all what makes the whole place so special.

The Via Francigena was also an important trade and military route because it links the Aosta Valley with the Vallesse region in Switzerland and the rest of Europe. The earliest records of inhabitants in the Aosta Valley relate to the Sassari, a Celtic tribe, who controlled both the Great St Bernard Pass to the north and the Little St Bernard Pass to the east, which links La Thuile in the Aosta Valley with Haute-Tarantaise in the Savoy region in France. When the Romans arrived in the Aosta Valley, they founded the city of Aosta in 25 BC and took control of the same passes. The Sassari had already settled along the River Dora Baltea, which runs across the middle of the region and from which other valleys lead off into the mountains. The Romans did the same and named their newly founded city Augusta Praetoria Salassorum (Aosta) after Emperor Augustus. From here, they crossed the Great St Bernard Pass to get to Northern Europe. This was also the route the Romans took out of Italy when Emperor Claudius sent his troops off to conquer Britannia in AD 43. At the time it was part of the Roman route known as Via delle Gallie (Way of the Gauls), which linked Rome with the Rhône Valley in France.

It's difficult not to be affected by mountains such as these, and especially if you live here. Chat to the people who live near Monte Bianco and they will speak to you affectionately about Il Bianco or 'the White One', which forms the backdrop to their lives. Of course, you don't have to physically climb the mountains to enjoy them. After all, some of these mountains are 4000m and above. Luckily there are other options. Both the Skyway Monte Bianco and the Matterhorn Alpine Crossing give you the chance to get up close to some of Europe's most impressive mountains from the comfort of a cable car. It goes without saying that the views are spectacular. This is the stuff you dream about for years afterwards.

One thing you'll notice when you visit is that the region has two languages. At one time the Aosta Valley belonged to the region of Savoy, but then in 1860 the Treaty of Turin made the County of Nice and the Duchy of Savoy French, while the Aosta Valley became part of the Kingdom of Sardinia, just before the Unification of Italy in 1861. This meant that an area that spoke the Franco-Provençal dialect and shared the Provençal culture became part of Italy. Nowadays the Aosta Valley has bilingual status and has done since 1948, when it became an autonomous region.

EARLY ALPINISM

Wherever there are mountains, there is a history of alpinism. Jacques Balmat and Michel-Gabriel Paccard made the first recorded ascent up Mont Blanc on 8 August 1786. They left Chamonix over the border in France, slept overnight on the Montagne de la Côte and reached the summit through severe winds in early evening. After two years of trying, they had finally made it. On 13 August 1863, three guides from Courmayeur, Julien Grange, Adolphe Orset and Jean-Marie Perrod, made the first successful expedition from the Italian side. In the meantime, women had been making their mark. Marie Paradis, a young waitress from Chamonix, reached the summit on 14 July 1808. She wasn't an alpinist

Courmayeur. DroneView / Adobe Stock

and had no experience of climbing mountains or of high altitudes. Her reason for wanting to climb Mont Blanc was purely practical. She thought that the fame it would bring her would earn her a more lucrative living serving food in Courmayeur as the woman who climbed Mont Blanc.[1] It took her three days of hellish difficulties with the help of local guides. She made it to the top, came back down, and gained her fame as Marie of Mont Blanc.[2] Henriette D'Angeville, a French aristocrat from

Geneva and a passionate mountaineer, reached the summit on 3 September 1838. She is often said to be the first woman mountaineer in history and was given the title of the 'Bride of Mont Blanc'.[3]

Interest in alpinism grew and on 23 October 1863 the Italian Alpine Club or Club Alpino Italiano (CAI) was founded in Turin. Its objectives were alpinism, the knowledge and study of mountains, and the protection of the natural environments involved. If today there is a network of mountain refuges and bivouacs in the mountains, it is because of the work of CAI over the years.

LOCAL FOOD

The Aosta Valley is famous for its *salumi* (cured meats) and cheeses. *Jambon de Bosses* is the local ham. You'll also find *mocetta*, a type of cold smoked beef that's flavoured with herbs and salt. Also look out for the famous *Lardo d'Arnad*, which is served in slices. This is the only *lardo* (lard) that has European DOP status or protected designated origin. With regards to cheese, try the local *Fontina*. It's matured for at least three months and in summer it's made with the milk from cows which have grazed on the mountain pastures. *Bleu d'Aoste* is a blue cheese with a stronger flavour and reminiscent of French blue cheeses. Local dishes include *gnocchi alla bava*, *gnocchi* made with *Fontina* cheese, potatoes served with pears and *fonduta alla valdostana*, fondue with *Fontina* cheese. *Tegole* are the traditional biscuits, made with nuts and almonds.

Local cheeses. Rachael Martin

Skyway Monte Bianco

The Skyway Monte Bianco takes you up to 3,466m for views of Monte Bianco and the Dente del Gigante (Dent du Géant or Giant's Tooth) up close. It's a feat of engineering with rotating cable cars that give you an all-round view above the clouds. Take the Skyway at the Skyway Courmayeur/The Valley station just outside Courmayeur. Go up to Pavillon/The Mountain at 2,173m first to get used to the altitude before going higher. Visit the botanical gardens at the Giardino Botanico Sausserrea, with its collection of plants from all over the world and check for eventual exhibitions. Then get back on and go up to Hellbronner/The Sky.[4] It's certainly an unforgettable way of visiting one of the world's most famous mountains, and an extremely memorable day out.

www.montebianco.com

View of Mont Blanc from up at The Sky, Skyway Monte Bianco. Rachael Martin

Matterhorn Alpine Crossing

The Matterhorn Alpine Crossing links Breuil-Cervinia in Italy to Zermatt in Switzerland and is the highest continuous Alpine crossing by cable car. The Matterhorn Glacier Paradise is the highest mountain station in Europe up at 3,833. It's surrounded by over thirty-eight mountains above 4,000m and a total of fourteen glaciers in France, Italy and Switzerland.[5] The cable cars with their see-through floors mean that you can enjoy the views around you and below.

www.matterhornparadise.ch

The Matterhorn, or Monte Cervino as it's known in Italian. bigterry / Adobe Stock

THE PILGRIMAGE

To understand the Via Francigena, we need to firstly look at the pilgrimage. In the Middle Ages there were three major destinations for pilgrimages: the Holy Land, where Christ's crucifixion, burial and resurrection are believed to have taken place; Santiago de Compostela and its cathedral, where the Apostle Saint James is buried; and Rome, home of the tombs of the apostles Saint Peter and Saint Paul. The Via Francigena led to Rome, along with other European routes known as the Via Romea Germanica and the Via Romea Strata, a modern route which joins together the routes that people used in the past and that brings pilgrims from the east of Europe. These are considered the three major routes to Rome. Romea meant that the road went to Rome, while the pilgrims themselves were known as Romers. Those going to the Holy Land were known as Palmers.

Jorge Anastacio / Adobe Stock

From Rome you could continue along the Via Appia, a Roman road built under the direction of statesman Appius Claudius Caecus. It connected Rome with the port of Brindisi in Puglia, where you took a boat to Greece and then continued on to the Holy Land. Brindisi was the second most important port after Venice and one of the gateways to the east. It was also where the crusaders set off to the Holy Lands, including those on the First Crusade at the end of the eleventh century.

During the Middle Ages, both church and religion were a central part of life, and if you wanted to be a good Christian, you went on a pilgrimage. The physical journey was also a spiritual journey, and the aim was to bring you closer to God and ultimately gain you less time in purgatory and your place in heaven. Some went as an act of penance to seek forgiveness for their sins. People were also sent on pilgrimages. After all, you could meet bandits or wild animals along the way, get lost and never be found, or quite simply die of illness along the way. There was always the possibility that you might not come back.[6] Sometimes it was a way to ask for healing or a favour from God. The Middle Ages was also the time of the Plague across Europe, and some travelled on pilgrimages to escape or ask for deliverance from it.

The classic story of the medieval pilgrimage is that of Geoffrey Chaucer's

The Canterbury Tales, written at the end of the fourteenth century, a series of twenty-four tales told by twenty-four pilgrims. It emphasises the fact that pilgrims often gathered in groups. This was mainly a question of safety, but as Chaucer shows it enabled people from all walks of life to spend time together, in contrast to their daily lives which often kept them apart. Obviously, all Chaucer's characters could afford to go on the pilgrimage in the first place. Pilgrimages weren't for the poor as it cost money to travel, find lodgings and pay for guides, all of which could prove expensive. In Chaucer's tales we have characters such as a knight, a miller and the wife of Bath. Chaucer's pilgrimage ends at Canterbury Cathedral, whereas the Via Francigena begins at Canterbury Cathedral. This spirit of people gathering and meeting as they walk continues today. Walking the Via Francigena or any other pilgrimage today may or may not necessarily be an act of faith, but just as in Chaucer's time, it's a moment where people meet from all walks of life and are united by a shared purpose.

If you were leaving England on the way to Rome, the first difficulty you had to overcome was crossing the English Channel. After that you went across France and into what we now call Italy via the Alps. If you were walking the Via Francigena, this took you over the Great St Bernard Pass. Crossing mountain passes was at one time the only way over from northern Europe into Italy. When Napoleon invaded in 1800, it was via the Great St Bernard Pass. The Aosta Valley is a region of castles, and it then took him another two weeks to take control of and get past the Castle of Bard. In the years of feudalism, castles were both a method of defence and a symbol of power. The Alpine State of Savoy, of which the Aosta Valley was once part, controlled the routes and collected the tolls. As with any trade route, it was a profitable business.

VIA FRANCIGENA: THE ROUTE

The Via Francigena starts in Canterbury Cathedral in Canterbury, Kent, England, specifically beside the south porch where you'll find the kilometre zero stone and can get your special Pilgrim's Credential. From there it's an onward journey to Dover and over to Calais into France, through the regions of Champagne-Ardenne and Franche-Comtè. Then it's on into Switzerland and along Lake Geneva towards the Alps and the Great St Bernard Pass and over the border into Italy. There are forty-five stages on the Italian stretch, which pass through seven regions: the Aosta Valley, Piedmont, Lombardy, Emilia-Romagna, Liguria, Tuscany and Lazio where you finally reach Rome. The whole walk is around 850km. It passes through towns and villages such as Aosta, Vercelli, Pavia, Piacenza, Fidenza, Lucca, San Gimignano, Monteriggioni,

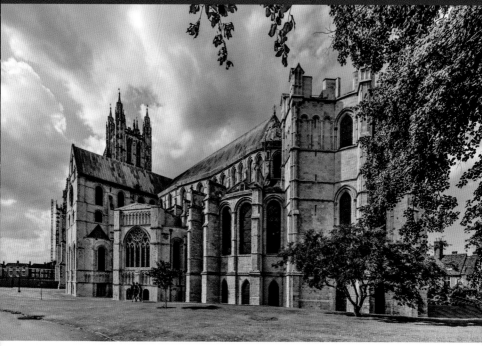

Canterbury Cathedral. Paul Regitnig / Adobe Stock

Siena and Viterbo, through the landscapes of the Alps, the Po Valley and the Appenines, the now-extinct ancient volcanoes of Val d'Orca, and finally to Rome.

The Italian route grew up around the Via di Monte Bardone. Monte Bardone was named after Mons Longobardorum, the Roman name for the Passo della Cisa, which links the Ligurian Appenines with the Appenines of Tuscany and Emilia-Romagna. The Franks then named it Via Francigena when they took over from the Longobards in the eighth century. Charlemagne, the Frankish king, was the Emperor of the Holy Roman Empire and a devout Christian, and what had once been a trade route now also become a way for pilgrims. What we know about the Via Francigena today is thanks to Sigeric, Archbishop of Canterbury. According to the Old English annals *The Anglo-Saxon Chronicle*, Sigeric travelled to Rome in 990, around the time when pilgrimages were starting to become popular. He went to receive the pallium from Pope John XV. The pallium is literally the narrow white liturgical vestment which rests on a bishop's shoulders around his neck. It's made of wool to show the bishop as a good shepherd, a reference to Christ as the Lamb of God who was sacrificed for humankind.[7] On his way back, Sigeric wrote what would today be called a travel diary. In it he recorded the churches he visited and the eighty-seven stops he made on his way from Rome to Canterbury.[8] In writing down his journey, he was giving others a guide to follow the same route and undertake the same pilgrimage to Rome. It was a type of medieval travel guide for pilgrims, providing you could read it of course. The vast majority of people could not.

The Via Francigena was named a Cultural Route of the Council of Europe in 1994 because of its role in joining together Anglo-Saxon and Latin cultures and bringing the whole of Europe together. When you walk the Via Francigena, you're also re-discovering the cultural roots of Europe. The route was extended from Rome to Santa Maria Leuca in 2019 according to what is written in the *Itinerarium Burdigalense*, a Latin text from 333. It's another kind of travel diary written by an anonymous pilgrim who is believed to have started out in Bordeaux and reached Santa Maria Leuca on the most southern tip of Puglia.[9] The whole route from Canterbury to Santa Maria de Leuca is over 3,000km long.

In 1985 anthropologist Giovanni Castelli started writing a book about walking in Italy and was looking for inspiration. He came upon the Via Francigena. He did the whole walk from Canterbury to Rome and recorded it as he went, just as Sigeric had done

The Pilgrim's Credential

The Pilgrim's Credential was a document given to pilgrims during the Middle Ages by the parish priest or bishop. It served as official proof that the person in question was on a pilgrimage and to safeguard the pilgrim on his or her journey. Today, the Credential has a similar purpose as it shows that the individual has walked either the whole pilgrimage or certain stretches of it. It can also get you a discount at hostels and certain restaurants. You should always check the relevant information thoroughly on each walk's site and make sure you leave plenty of time to apply for it before you go. For some pilgrim accommodation, you will need the Credential to stay there, so always ask when you book. The Testimonium, proof that you have walked the way in question, is dependent on either walking the whole walk or a certain number of kilometres in the case of longer walks. For the Via Francigena, this is at least 100km.

a thousand years before. The whole of the route was retraced according to Sigeric's original document, with necessary variations according to how urbanisation and roads and motorways had built up over the years, and maps were drawn up by the Italian Military Geographical Institute. This is the route that you can travel today, inspired by that of Sigeric a thousand years ago.

CROSSING THE GREAT ST BERNARD PASS

This first stage of the Italian route takes you to Echevennoz in the Great St Bernard Valley below. It's just under 15km and is of medium difficulty because the route begins up in the high mountains. But firstly, a bit of history.

If we look back at the origins of the Via Francigena, we can see that it was the Romans who first built a road through the valley up over Mons Jovis, as they called the pass, on their way over the Alps to conquer Britannia. They considered the pass to be sacred, dedicated it to Jupiter Poeninus and built a temple. They named the mountain plateau here Plan de Jupiter. The archaeological site here has remains of the temple and two other buildings that were part of a *mansio* (rest station or road station) and were discovered in the nineteenth century. It's thought that before then the Celts came here and built a temple to their

Great St Bernard Pass. Rachael Martin

own god, Penn, and that even further back people from the Bronze Age came here.

The Great St Bernard Hospice, just over the border in Switzerland, is where pilgrims rested, slept and ate. The original hospice was founded in 1045 by Saint Bernard of Montjoux, Archdeacon of the Cathedral of Aosta. He also founded the hospice at the Little St Bernard Pass on the Italy-France border, which links La Thuile with Val d'Isère. Crossing the mountains could be dangerous, not only because of natural dangers but because there were bandits up in the mountains and travellers risked attacks. Hospices offered pilgrims a place of safety, a decent meal and a place to sleep. The Statue of Saint Bernard above the lake has been there since 1929 after Pope Pius XI made him patron saint of the Alps in 1923. This is a place with strong links to Christianity and it's this that makes the whole place so special.

In the sixteenth century, the Counts of Savoy granted exclusive rights to the people of Saint-Rhémy-en-Bosses and neighbouring Étroubles to accompany travellers through the valley from Aosta and over the Great St Bernard Pass. These people were known as *maronniers* or mountain guides and became part of the Maronniers et Soldats de la Neige who later became the famous Guide Alpini, the official Alpine mountain guides. At one point

it was thought that Hannibal passed over here with his army mounted on horses and elephants on his way to conquer Rome. Recent evidence, however, suggests that Hannibal and his troops passed into Italy via the Colle delle Traversette, the pass leading into Piedmont from France. Mountain passes have always represented both opportunity and danger of attack. When Napoleon went over the pass, through snow and ice in May 1800, the monks at the Hospice are reported to have fed some of the soldiers. He then went on to fight the Battle of Marengo on 14 June where he won against the Austrians. Napeoleon up at the Great St Bernard Pass was immortalised in the painting *Napoleon crossing the Alps* by Jacques-Louis David.

The Hospice here is run by the religious community The Congregation of the Canons of Saint Bernard. You can visit the church and the museum which traces the history of the pass, its spiritual significance over the years, and those who passed through it. There's also a shop where you can buy books, maps and souvenirs. What you'll probably also notice is the Saint Bernard dog soft toys. The Hospice is also famous for the Saint Bernard mountain-rescue dogs, that were also used to guard the monks there. You can visit the kennels which the Barry Foundation use in summer for their dogs. You might also see the dogs out on their walks while you're there.

From the Great St Bernard Pass to Echevennoz

One of the most evocative ways of doing the walk is to do as the medieval pilgrim might have done and spend a night at the Great St Bernard Hospice. The monks of the time were renowned for their hospitality. Saint Benedict of Norcia insisted on hospitality in accordance with Christ's example when he wrote his Rule of Saint Benedict in 530. Saint Benedict was the saint who established monasteries as physical places with abbots, in contrast with the concept of individual hermits and wanderers that had been usual previously. As a result of the Benedictine Rule, monasteries grew up all over Europe and monks and nuns offered food and lodging to pilgrims, travellers, nobles and even royalty. To do so was to follow the teachings of Christ.

It's an incredible feeling as you leave the Hospice and walk over the border into Italy along the old mule track 103 towards Italy with the lake on your left. The views of the mountains and of Grand Combin (4,314m) as you make your way down are impressive. It's the kind of place where you just want to stop, take your time and soak it all up. After making your way down the mountain, you'll visit several

Statue of Saint Bernard at the Great St Bernard Pass. Bombast / Adobe Stock

Above: *Saint-Rhémy-en-Bosses.* e55evu / Adobe Stock

Left: *Étroubles.* Gabriele Bignoli / Adobe Stock

villages. The first is Saint-Rhémy-en-Bosses (signposted as Saint-Rhémy), with its grey stone houses that are characteristic of the villages in the valley. In Roman times it had a *mansio*, a place where travellers could rest and change horses. It's famous for its ham *Jambon de Bosses*, a type of *prosciutto crudo* that has DOP status. It also has the ferruginous water of the Citrin spring, which you can find at the fountain in the square in front of the town hall. If you're feeling hungry, stop off at the Prosciutteria Sous le Pont de Bosses, where the garage is. They're specialists in the local ham, as well as other dishes such as raclette. They also have a shop where you can pick up ham and bread for sandwiches later. Saint-Rhémy has two major walks which go through it. The first is obviously the Via Francigena. The second is the Via Alpina, which links the whole of the Alps from one end to the other. This international project offers five trails and goes across eight countries: Monaco, France, Italy, Switzerland, Lichtenstein, Germany, Austria and Slovenia. It's over 15,000km long, has 342 stages, and takes you up to a height of 3,000m. The 2017 documentary *Via Alpina: Beyond the Trail* tells the 5,000km solo journey of documentary maker Matthieu Chambaud. For information about the Via Alpina, and a list of maps and guidebooks, see **www.via-alpina.org**.

After leaving Saint-Rhémy, continue to Saint Leonard. The Castello di Bosses here was built by the Lords of Bosses in the twelfth century, rebuilt in the fifteenth century, and now hosts events and temporary exhibitions. Saint Oyen is the next village, followed by Étroubles, one of Italy's most beautiful villages or *borghi* as they're known in Italian. Étroubles has an open-air art museum with works by internationally famous artists distributed around the village. It's part of a project with the Giannada Foundation over the border in Martigny, which began in 2005. Étroubles is a charming village and beautifully kept, with typical stone houses from the area with their geraniums outside, narrow streets and drinking fountains where you can drink the water that comes down from Mont Vélan. Always look out for the geraniums. Nowhere do they grow as well as in the mountains. There are five chapels around the village, proof of how much faith mattered in these remote villages. The village also boasts a communal oven where the local black bread was always cooked in November, left to dry and kept for the whole year.

After Étroubles, you come to Echevennoz, which marks the end of your walk. You could always get up the next day and do the next stage to Aosta and spend a night there. It's a downhill walk along the Ru Neuf, the irrigation canal that runs through the Great St Bernard Valley and passes through the village of Gignod. It's picture postcard perfect with the view of its church set against the mountain of Grand Combin. For further information, see the links below.

Eat
Étroubles
La Croix Blanche
The restaurant is housed in what was an inn for travellers four centuries ago. Look out for their *zuppa alla valpellinese*, the local soup which takes its name after the nearby valley the Valpelline. It's made with black bread, *Fontina* cheese and cabbage.

Ristorante La Croix Blanche, Route Nationale du Grand Saint Bernard, 10 www.croixblanche.it

Trattoria Marietty

This family-run trattoria has been here since the beginning of the twentieth century with traditional dishes, homemade cakes and local wines.

Trattoria Marietty
Hameau de Echevennoz, 3
www.trattoriamarietty.it

Saint-Rhémy-en-Bosses
Prosciutteria Sous le Pont de Bosses

A prosciutteria is where you can buy and eat ham, and in this case lots of local dishes too. Enjoy the famous *Jambon de Bosses* ham and more and stock up with goodies from the deli for your journey.

Prosciutteria Sous le Pont de Bosses, località Predumaz Falcoz

Stay

Your Credential (or Pilgrim's Passport) will give you discounts at various structures. For some structures you will need it. The idea is that you also collect stamps as you go along, so it also serves as an official record of your journey. See the official website www.viefrancigine.org for details on how to obtain it.

Étroubles
Ostello Dortoir

The Ostello Dortoir is in the early eighteenth century chapel, the Cappella di Echevennoz, and is run by the same family who own the Trattoria Marietty. It offers 18 beds in hostel style accommodation with breakfast. They also offer specific services for pilgrims and walkers such as laundry, information about weather conditions and so on. Please note that the hostel is closed between October and April.

Ostello Dortoir, Frazione Echevennoz
Email: ruffierdidier@libero.it

Great St Bernard Pass
Great St Bernard Hospice

If you want to really soak up the spiritual atmosphere up here in the mountains, this is the place to stay, just over the border in Switzerland. Accommodation is offered in dormitories or individual rooms.

Great St Bernard Hospice
www.gsbernard.com

Saint-Rhémy-en-Bosses
Nuit a Pleiney

This beautiful B&B run by Sara and Marco also has an apartment which sleeps four. They have a sauna and relaxation room which is perfect for after you've been walking and can provide a local aperitivo on request. Both Sara and Marco are very knowledgeable about the local area and are always happy to recommend further walks and activities such as e-bikes.

Nuit a Pleiney, 4, Loc, 11010 Saint-Rhémy-en-Bosses

While You're Here

- Visit the military fort Forte di Bard up on the rocky hill above the medieval village of Bard. It was rebuilt by the House of Savoy in the nineteenth century and is said to be one of the finest examples of its kind. It was also used as the setting for several scenes in *The Avengers: Age of Ultron*. **www.fortedibard.it**.

- Head to the Gran Paradiso National Park, Italy's oldest national park that was set up in 1922 and named after the mountain of the same name. There's plenty of walking along signposted trails both through the valleys and up the mountains. For further details, trails and maps see **www.pngp.it**

- Aosta is known as the Rome of the Alps, with its Arch of Augustus, Porta Pretoria, theatre, bridge and Roman walls. The city is still based on the original Roman plan. If you really want to appreciate the drama of this beautiful city, make sure to go there in the evening when it's all lit up. Find out more at **www.lovevda.it**

Forte di Bard. Franklyn / Adobe Stock

Gran Paradiso National Park.
Alessandro / Adobe Stock

Valpelline. Rachael Martin

- From Aosta you can walk to the Lo Tsatelet nature reserve. It's a popular place for birds during the migration season and is home to various mammals and reptiles. For details of the walk, see www.lovevda.it and look for 'Hiking to Lo Tsatelet nature reserve'.
- Walk along the Place du Moulin Dam in the valley of the Valpelline. The dam is one of the largest in Europe and an engineering feat, while the landscape is like something out of a fairy tale.
- Head to Saint-Oyen and its *Sagra del Prosciutto*, the local ham festival which takes place on the first weekend of August. Here you'll see hams being roasted over open fires with herbs, and then eaten with green beans or polenta.

Maps, Links and Useful Information
Aosta Valley
www.loveda.it is the official tourism website and is an excellent first point of call for checking out the region in general. Also see www.turisimovda.it and www.valledaosta-guidaturistica.it

Via Francigena
The official website is www.viefrancigene.org and includes routes, maps, guides, apps and practical information. Also download the app Via Francigena - Official App
www.loveda.it has useful information about the walk through the region, with estimated times and an extensive list of accommodation. See www.lovevda.it/en/sport/trekking/via-francigena
Also check out www.pilgrimstorome.org.uk for useful information and first-hand accounts.

When to go
The pass is closed in winter from mid-October and opens again in June in the annual joint Italian-Swiss ceremony. July and August tend to be the warmest months for walking up there.

Guides
Hire a guide to take you down from the mountain pass and explain the route as you walk. For local guides, write to Flavio Dalle at f.dalle63@gmail.com

GETTING HERE AND GETTING AROUND

The nearest airport is in Turin. Alternatively, Milan or Genoa are both options. It's then a train journey to Aosta, followed by a two-and-a-half to three-and-a-half-hour bus journey up to the pass. Alternatively, hire a car to fully make the most of exploring the area.

FROM MILAN TO LAKE COMO TO SWITZERLAND

→ Sentiero di Leonardo – Milan to Milan via Switzerland
→ Antica Via Regina – Como to Sorico
→ Strada Regia – Como to Bellagio
→ Sentiero del Viandante – Lecco to Colico
→ Via Francisca – Sorico to Chiavenna
→ Via Spluga – Chiavenna, Italy to Thusis, Switzerland

INTRODUCTION

Visitors have understood the attraction of Lake Como since Roman times. Pliny the Younger had several villas there, Wordsworth got lost walking above Gravedona and wrote about it in *The Prelude*, and George Clooney bought a lakeside villa in Laglio. Lake Como has everything you could desire for that perfect *dolce vita* experience: exclusive hotels, Liberty villas, lakeside villages with pastel-coloured houses, charming squares for lunch or aperitivo, and unforgettable views of a lake surrounded by mountains. If the stereotypes exist, it's for a reason. Yet to stick with the stereotypes would be only to see half a story, for there is so much more to Lake Como. The fact that it's surrounded by mountains means it has excellent walking opportunities. A glacial lake, it's Italy's deepest, and the fifth deepest lake in Europe. The way it cuts through the mountains is quite spectacular, and especially around Lecco, with its rocky mountains of Resegone and Grigna.

Look at a map of Lake Como and you'll see it starts off as one and then splits into two bifurcations at the promontory of Bellagio. The western bifurcation leads down to Como, while the eastern one leads down to Lecco. Lecco still has its bridge named after

Lecco, with Mount Resegone above it. Rachael Martin

Como. Boris Stroujko / Adobe Stock

Ponte Azzone Visconti, the fourteenth century duke who realised the town's strategic importance and strengthened links between Milan and Lecco. You'll often hear this side of the lake called Lake Lecco, particularly by the local *Lecchesi,* as the people of Lecco are known. The older name for Lake Como was Lake Lario, from the Latin *Larius,* which was what the Romans called it. It wasn't until the medieval period when it began to take on the name of Lake Como after the city of Como. Lecco is the point where you can go north to Switzerland, or south-east to the town of Bergamo. It's where the Viandante goes up to Colico. The Strada Antica Regina leaves from Como up to Sorico. The Via Francisca goes from Sorico up to Chiavenna. From Chiavenna, all roads lead to Switzerland.

Como, which still has its Roman grid layout, thrived during Roman times. Julius Caesar realised the strategic value of its position and founded the city in 59 BC. He called it Novum Comum. When the Romans left, it was attacked and occupied by the Goths, and later by the Longobards. Frederick Barbarossa was welcomed to Como in 1159 as an ally against the Milanese, but then in 1335 Como became part of the Duchy of Milan under the Duke Azzone Visconti. Fast forward a few more years and Leonardo da Vinci was living at the court of Milan at the end of the fifteenth century. The duke was Ludovico the Moor and the court lived at the Sforza Castle. Ludovico was also the duke who

encouraged the silk industry in Como. In the 1970s, when the Italian fashion industry took off in Milan, it was able to do so because of the local heritage of textile industries such as that of Como.

Climb up over the mountains along the western side of the Como stretch and you will reach Switzerland, just as members of the Italian Resistance did during the Second World War to take people to safety or to reach medical assistance. When you reach the top of Lake Como, just past Colico, you can go east and on to the Valtellina, or head north to the town of Chiavenna and the Valchiavenna and on to Switzerland. Take the road straight on from Chiavenna and you'll go through Val Bregaglia and up the Maloja Pass to St Moritz, again in Switzerland. The road to the left goes up to the Valle Spluga, a pocket of Italy surrounded on three sides by Switzerland. It crosses the Swiss border at Passo dello Spluga, or the Spluga Pass. The historical way up here is known as Via Spluga. Over the border is the Val Mescolina in Switzerland, linked to the Valle Spluga by walks over the mountains. The Valle Spluga is a wilder, lesser-known area of Italy, and all the more beautiful because of it.

Please note that for all the routes mentioned below, apart from the Via Antica Regina, the app Le Vie del Viandante is the one to download. It has routes, maps and plenty of useful information. The official tourist site of the Lombardy region is **www.in-lombardia.it**

SENTIERO DI LEONARDO

The Sentiero di Leonardo (Path of Leonardo) is 540km long and was designed in 2019, the 500th anniversary of his death. The purpose behind it was to give tourists the opportunity to enjoy some of the places associated with him and to rediscover his world. The route starts at the Alzaia della Martesana, along the path that follows the Naviglio della Martesana. The *navigli* (canals) were Milan's system of waterways. Da Vinci studied them while he was at the court of Ludovico the Moor and made Milan's canal system an engineering feat that was respected and admired throughout Europe. An *alzaia* was a path by the side of a canal where horses or donkeys walked and pulled the boats along the canal. In Milan there were five of these paths, one for each of the five canals, and Alzaia della Martesana was one.

Naviglio della Martesana. Copyright Comune di Milano

The path goes out of Milan to Trezzo sull'Adda, along the River Adda as far as Lecco and Lake Como. Then it's up to Chiavenna along the Sentiero del Viandante, up and over the Spluga Pass and down to Splügen in Switzerland, and then over the the San Bernardino pass. It then comes south again through Switzerland to Lugano, and then back down along the outskirts east of Milan. From Milan it goes to Pavia, and then back up to Milan again.

Leonardo da Vinci was the ultimate Renaissance man because he was so skilled and knowledgeable in so many fields. This walk shows exactly that. It takes you to over fifty places most associated with his genius, from the fields of engineering, the arts and the sciences. It also gives you the opportunity to explore five UNESCO sites such as the Church and Dominican Convent of Santa Maria delle Grazie in Milan, where you'll find da Vinci's *The Last Supper*. If you haven't been, it's one of Italy's most precious artistic treasures, although you will have to book in advance.

For information about the Sentiero di Leonardo see **www.leviedelvieandate.eu**. The section from Milan to Lecco is 78.6km, is classed as easy and can be done in four stages.

ANTICA VIA REGINA

The Antica Via Regina, or L'Antica Strada Regina, is 77km long and goes from Como to Sorico at the top of the lake. It's part of the system of walks and waterways that went up the lake and linked what we now know as Italy with the rest of Europe. Footpaths, mule tracks and waterways were the main routes up the lake, and it was because of this that villages grew up on the lake with their churches, stone houses, bridges and other historic treasures.[1] We have the first mention of a Via Regina in 1187. It's been suggested that the Latin term *via regina* has the same meaning as *via regia*, which referred to a road that belonged to a city state, kingdom or other governing body. These roads often followed Roman roads and were deemed an important means of communication between two places. In the case of the Antica Via Regina, Via Francisca, and Via Spluga to the north, they were all part of a series of routes that connected the two countries

From Gravedona to Domaso. Provincia di Como

we now know as Italy and Switzerland. Towards the end of the third century, Milan (or Mediolanum as it was called by the Romans) became the capital of the Roman Empire, and because of this Como (Comum) was extremely important strategically. Samoloco and Chiavenna at the north of the lake were also of strategic importance, as Chiavenna led both to the Julier Pass and the Spluga Pass and in both cases to Switzerland.[2] The Via Spluga led to Thusis and Chur in Switzerland. At the time Chur was capital of the Alpine Roman province known as Rezia or *Raetia* in Latin. It was made up of what today covers Alto Adige, southern Bavaria, part of Switzerland and western Austria. Link *Mediolanum* (Roman Milan) with Chur as the Romans did and you have an effective system of defence. You also have a network ready to facilitate trade.

Nowadays the Antica Via Regina is a mix of mule tracks, footpaths and roads. What makes it so enjoyable is that you're walking in the footsteps of history through some of the lake's most beautiful and much-loved villages. It sometimes feels a world apart from the usual Lake Como stereotypes of the glamourous *dolce vita* and quaint lakeside villages. It makes you aware of how much there is within the landscape of Lake Como, how much history and how many stories there are of its places and people. As you leave Como, there's Cernobbio, which is famous for its Villa d'Este. This sixteenth century villa was built by Pelligrino Pelligrini as Villa

Galovo for Tolomeo Gallio, who was Cardinal of Como at the time. In 1815 it became the property of Caroline of Brunswick, Princess of Wales and wife of George IV. The villa is now known as the Grand Hotel Villa d'Este.

Villa Erba was built at the end of the nineteenth century for the Erba family, on the grounds of where there was once a Benedictine monastery. In 1900 their daughter Carla married the wealthy and influential Giuseppe Visconti di Modrone, Duke of Grazzano Visconti. Their son was the Italian film and theatre director Luchino Visconti. Visconti was considered one of the most important artistic and cultural figures of the twentieth century, and this is where he spent many summers as a boy. It's said that the house served as a constant muse to him throughout his life. What was once a family summer house belonging to one of the most important families on the social scene in Milan is now an international congress centre where some of the world's most important politicians meet. Cernobbio is also where the Via dei Monti Lariani (Larian Mountain Trail) starts. It's part of the Sentiero Italia, the Great Italian Trail, and links Cernobbio with Sorico. Laglio dates back to Roman times and is where George Clooney bought his villa. Then there's Argegno and its old centre with the its church, the Chiesa di Santa Trinità and the village of Tremezzo. The Villa Carlotta here took its name after Carlotta, daughter of Marianna of Prussia, when it was given to her as a wedding present in 1850. The pretty village of Menaggio is one of the most popular villages on the lake and is where the boats leave for Varenna and Bellagio. The route continues all the way up to the north of the lake and the villages of Dongo, Domaso and Gravedona. The mountains of the Valtellina and the Valchiavenna beckon in the distance and the air is pierced with the wind known as the Breva. It's no accident that this part of the lake is famous for watersports such as kite surfing.

Bear in mind that part of the Via Antica Regina goes along roads. These are busy roads often without footpaths and you should get on a bus along these stretches. One of the most beautiful stretches of the route is that from Menaggio to Santa Maria Mezzonico. It's 9km long and takes roughly three hours. For maps and details of the walk, see www.viedelviadante.eu or download the app.

For maps of The Larian Mountain Trail, see www.leviedelviandate.eu

Eat
Como
Vintage Jazz Food and Wine
Set in a square in the historical centre of Como, the bar specialises in wine, cocktails and food. It's the perfect atmosphere to while away those summer evenings after a day's walking.

Via Olginati, 14
www.vintagejazzcomo.com

Trattoria Il Solito Posto
The trattoria is in the historic centre in what were once fifteenth century stables, and serves typical dishes from the area.

Via Lambertenghi, 9
www.ilsolitoposto.net

Menaggio
Trattoria La Vecchia Magnolia
If you're wanting a day's rest from walking and a leisurely lunch, this is the place to go. It's slightly out of Menaggio in Leveno, and serves lake fish and dishes from the Valtellina.

Via Per Plesio, 6
www.trattorialavecchiamagnolia.it

Stay
Como
In Riva al Lago
In Riva al Lago is in the centre of Como, 50m from buses and boats that go up the lake. It has its own El Merendero pub with pasta, salads, panini, pizzas and around fifty international beers.

Via Benedetto e Maria Crespi, 4
www.inrivaallago.com
www.elmerenderocomo.it

Ostello Bello
Ostello Bello Como is run by the same people who opened Ostello Bello in Milan in 2010. It's in the centre of Como, ten minutes from the station and reception is open 24 hours. It has indivudal, shared and family rooms, all

with bathrooms. They also have a bar and outside garden.

Viale Fratelli Rosselli, 9
www.ostellobello.com

Menaggio
Hotel Garni Corona
Hotel Garni Corona is a three-star hotel in the main square of Menaggio with views of the lake. It's also five minutes away from both bus stop and the landing stage for the boat service that goes up and down the lake.

Largo Cavour, 3
www.hotelgarnicorona.com

Lake Como Hostel La Primula
The hostel is near the lake and offers bed and breakfast. It also has its own restaurant. Accommodation is in twin and double rooms, shared rooms and all male, all female and mixed dormitories. Staff organise rock climbing, kayaking, Italian language lessons and sailing on request.

Via IV November, 106
www.lakecomohostel.com

While You're Here
- Walk west in Como along the lakeside promenade known as the Passeggiata Lino Gelpi to see the Liberty style Villa Saporiti and Villa Gallia. Villa Olmo is neoclassical in style with Liberty style interiors.
- Take the 1894 funicular from Piazza Gasperi 700m up to Brunate, the mountain plateau above Como known as the 'Balcony of the Alps'. There's plenty to see including Liberty villas and the Faro Voltiano, the Voltian lighthouse. It was built in 1927 on the 100th anniversary of Alessandro Volta's death. Climb up the 143 steps and enjoy the views. The Passeggiata delle Baite is a walk which takes you up into the mountains to several mountain refuges. It leaves from Piazzale del Cao.
- Get the boat from Como to Bellagio and visit the beautiful gardens of Villa Melzi, famous for its collection of camellias which flower between March and April. www.giardinidivillamelzi.it There are plenty of walking opportunities around above Bellagio. For trails, see www.bellagiolakecomo.com and for boat times see www.navigazionelaghi.it
- Isola Comacina is the lake's only island. In the medieval period it was an important religious centre and famous for churches such as that of Saint Euphemius, which was built by Litigerius in 1031. The people of Isola Comacina gave their allegiance to Milan, and because of this the island was destroyed by

View of Como from Brunate.
Provincia di Como

Isola Comacina. Provincia di Como

Como with the help of Frederick Barbarossa in 1169. Those who could fled across the water to Varenna. The island remained a ruin for centuries, until it was left to the king of Belgium, who then returned it to Italy. Look out for the 1930s artists' houses, designed by Pietro Lingeri, which were built with the idea of turning the island into a colony for artists. The island never did become a colony for artists, but the houses are still here. For information about the island see www.isola-comacina.it

- Remember the scene in *Star Wars: Attack of the Clones* where Anakin Skywalker kisses Padme in the garden? It was filmed at Villa del Balbianello, the eighteenth century villa at the end of the woody promontory Dosso di Lavedo further up from Isola Comacina. Visit the villa and take a walk about the gardens, known for their statues and wisteria plants.

Maps, Links and Useful Information
Como
The official website for Lake Como is www.lakecomo.is

The official website for Como is visitcomo.eu

Also check out the region's official website www.in-lombardia.it

Antica Via Regina

See camminidilombardia.it/via-regina for information and maps of all sections of the Antica Via Regina.

mylakecomo.co/en/attractions/antica-strada-regina also has information and maps for the section between Menaggio and Santa Maria Mezzonico.

Mussolini and Dongo

In 1945 Mussolini tried to flee along the Via Antica Regina leading up from Como. He was disguised as a German officer and with his lover Clara Petacci, within a German column that was directed towards Germany. The column was stopped at a roadblock on 27 April 1945 by a group of partisan fighters who were part of the 52nd Garibaldi Brigade which was active in the area. His identity was soon established, and he and Clara Petacci were taken to Palazzo Manzi, the town hall. The next day both Mussolini and Petacci were taken up to Giulino di Mezzagra and shot. Their bodies were then taken to Milan and hung in Piazzale Loreto on 29 April. The Museo della Fine della Guerra in Dongo has documentation and film of these days at the end of the Second World War in Italy.

www.museofineguerradongo.it

menaggio.com also has information and maps for the Menaggio - Santa Maria Mezzonico stretch.

For boat times see navigazionelaghi.it

When to go

You can pretty much walk the path all year round, apart from if there's snow in winter. Avoid July and August as it can get very hot and very busy. Both spring and autumn are perfect, although check in advance for hotels and restaurants as some places do close after the summer season.

LOCAL FOOD

Lake Como is famous for its dishes using freshwater fish. *Missoltini* or *misultin* in the local dialect are dried *agoni*, a bit like dried herrings, which are deboned, dipped in salt, left to dry in the sun for around five days and then conserved in vinegar. They are then grilled and often served with polenta. *Lavarello in carpione* are whitefish which are first fried in flour (minus their heads and tails) and then conserved in water and vinegar. *Risotto al pesce persico* uses perch in a traditional risotto finished with grated lemon peel. Local cheeses include *taleggio, robiola and quartirola* from Valsassina, and small round fresh or matured goat's cheeses known as *caprini*. The polenta here is either corn polenta with butter and cheese called *polenta uncia*, or *polenta taragna* which uses both

Grilled* missoltini *with polenta. Comugnero Silvana / Adobe Stock

cornflour and buckwheat flour and is served with butter and cheese. You'll also find *pizzoccheri*, buckwheat pasta cooked with potatoes and cabbage and mixed with butter and cheese.

STRADA REGIA

The Strada Regia is 35km long and links Como with Bellagio. It was originally a Roman road, and then a series of footpaths and mule tracks halfway up the mountain which linked the villages along the lake and was given the name Via Regia. It's said that Pope Urbino II came here in 1095 on his way to the Council of Clermont in Aquitaine, which

led to the First Crusade. The route was used by farmers, traders and travellers until they built the road along the lake at the beginning of the twentieth century, some of which follows the old mule track. It remained unused until 2002 when a project began to open it up again to walkers. To get to the start, take the funicular up to Brunate above Como, where the walk starts outside the station. It goes past the villages along the lake as far as the Ponte del Diavolo on the border between Lezzeno and Bellagio. From here, get a bus for the last two kilometres to Bellagio as it's a busy road without foothpaths and not suitable for walkers. Highlights

Strada Regia. Rachael Martin

Nesso. Camera Commercio Como Lecco

include the village of Nesso with its *orrido* (waterfall), which divides the village in two. The walk also passes through the hamlet of Palanzo above Fagetto Lario, known for its 1572 wine press known as the Torchio di Palanzo. In the past all this area was agricultural, and the wine press crushed the grapes for all.

For further information about the Strada Regia, see the viedelviandante.eu website and Le Vie del Vieandate app.

SENTIERO DEL VIANDANTE / THE WAYFARER'S PATH

The beginning of Alessandro Manzoni's novel *The Betrothed* opens with a description of the eastern arm of Lake Como, Lake Lecco. It's all in there in that opening paragraph, the lake which goes south in between two chains of mountains, various details of bridges and shore, the rivers, mountains and valleys, until you reach Lecco and the streets where the people are walking and going about their business. Dante is the father of the modern Italian language, while Manzoni gave Italy its first great novel and in doing so unified the Italian language. The novel was published in three parts between 1825 and 1827. It's a historical novel, set in Lecco and along Lake Lecco, and the betrothed couple Renzo and Lucia are one of the most famous couples in

Lake Como, view from Varenna. Rachael Martin

Italian literature. Manzoni was born in Milan, but he spent his adolescence between Milan and the family villa in Lecco. He knew the lake, Lecco and Mount Resegone, which takes its name from the Italian *sega* or saw because of the way it stretches across in a series of peaks, just like the blade of a saw. He knew the Grigna mountain range and the villages of Abbadia Lariana, Mandello del Lario, Varenna, Bellano and Colico. The mountains are rocky and steep as far as Varenna as they still form part of the Grigna range. It's no surprise that Lecco is internationally famous for its climbing club known as I Ragni (the Spiders).

The Viandante or the Wayfarer's Path goes from Lecco to Colico and is 49km long. It's part of the system of routes that links Milan and all the towns out towards Lecco with the Valtellina and Valchiavenna and the mountain passes of Spluga, Julier and Septimer, all of which lead into Switzerland. The route was designed in 1992 when the Azienda di Promozione Turistica del Lecchese joined together the Via Ducale and the Via Regia, which linked the northern part of the Duchy of Milan with the Fort of Fuentes in Colico. It was also known as the Via Napoleona when works were done to widen the path during the Napoleonic Age (1805-1814). Not that Napoleon's troops ever marched along here. This was a narrow mule track which was mainly used by locals. The main route from Lecco to the Valtellina and Valchiavenna passed through the valley above Lecco known as the Valsassina, and via Bellano at the top of the lake, until the lakeside road was built between 1824 and 1832.

Walk along the Viandante and you are immediately struck by its sheer beauty and the views of the lake below. The track is split into eight sections: Lecco to Abbadia, Abbadia to Lierna, Lierna to Varenna, Varenna to Dervio, and Dervio to Colico. It's classed as easy. Rather than walking up the mountains, you are walking along them. It's always advisable to wear trekking shoes or walking boots, though, as there are a few sections which are steep. From Colico you can continue to Sorico across the Pian di Spagna, a further 11.5km which takes you to the start of the Via Francisca and on to Chiavenna.

From Varenna to Dervio

The most beautiful stretch of the Viandante is said to be that from Varenna to Dervio, and it certainly gives you those fantastic views of the lake. It also gives you the perfect excuse to visit the village of Varenna. Spend the night there and give yourself the opportunity to soak it all up, including those sunsets, then get up early and walk to the piazza up in Vezio and the Castello di Vezio where your section of the walk begins. The walk is 12.5km long and is indicated as suitable for

Walking along the Viandante. Rachael Martin

tourists and hikers. It takes you via the hamlet of Perledo to the valley of Biosio where you could stop for lunch at the Crotto di Biosio. It's then on to Bellano, past the chapel Cappella della Madonna Addolorata. You then cross the bridge over the Pioverna stream and get to the Church of San Rocco in Bellano. The Orrido di Bellano is the narrow gorge which attracts so many to the town, while the town's lakefront has cafés where you can sit and enjoy the views of the surrounding mountains. If you want to get an insight into the life of the lake as it was, then read the novels of Andrea Vitali, who

was born there. After Bellano the path goes towards the hamlets of Ombriaco, Lezzeno, and Oro with wonderful views of the lake. The walk ends in Dervio at the Torre di Orezia, the remaining tower of what was once a medieval castle.

Castles along the Viandante

The castles along the Viandante give a fascinating insight into the area's history and are also a great way to approach parts of the walk with children. Lecco's Torre Viscontea (Visconti Tower) in the corner of Piazza XX Settembre is what's left of the impressive fourteenth century

Castello di Vezio, Varenna. nejdetduzen / Adobe Stock

castle built by Azzone Visconti, Duke of Milan. Visconti took Lecco in 1335 and built both the castle and the Ponte Azzone Visconti, also known as Ponte Vecchio or the old bridge. He was very much aware of Lecco's strategic position between Milan and the Valtellina.

Torre Viscontea, Lecco, opening hours: Thursday 10am-1pm, Friday to Sunday 2pm to 6pm.

The Torre di Maggiana in the hamlet of Maggiana above Mandello del Lario is one of the best-preserved medieval towers along the lake. It's also known as the Torre del Barbarossa as local legend says that the Germanic king Frederick Barbarossa stayed here on his way to attack Milan. **www.museotorremaggiana.it**

Legend tells us that Queen Theodolinda, the sixth century Longobard queen, built the Castello di Vezio above Varenna to defend the lake and its villages from invaders. The building we can see today dates from the eleventh century, a time when the people of Como often attacked Varenna because of its allegiance to Milan. The village was destroyed by Como in 1126. It was around this time that the people of the Island of Comacina on the Como branch of the lake took refuge here. They also gave their allegiance to Milan and so in 1169 their island was attacked and destroyed by Frederick Barbarossa. Barbarossa was welcomed by the people of Como. Look out for the daily falconry exhibitions which take place here. **www.castellodivezio.it**

The fourteenth century Castello di Orezia in Dervio had to defend itself against the Repubblica dei Tre Pievi, which lasted from the late twelfth century to the early sixteenth century. *Pieve* means church or religious district. In this case, it referred to those of Dongo, Gravedona and Sorico further north on the other side of the lake. Only the tower remains today. The Castello di Corenno Plinio is situated in the medieval hamlet of Corenno Plinio, part of Dervio. It was given in freehold to Fossato Andreani in 1271 by the Archbishop of Milan Ottone Visconti in return for his allegiance. The church was built by the Andreani family and dedicated to Thomas à Becket of Canterbury, who had been assassinated several years before. Frescoes inside the church date from between the fourteenth and sixteenth centuries. www.corenno.it

The sixteenth century Forte De Fuentes is in Colico. Milan was ruled by the Spanish between 1525 and 1700, and the fort was built by Pedro Enriquez de Acevedo, Governor of the State of Milan. Nearby nature reserve Pian di Spagna takes its name from the Spanish as *Spagna* means Spain in Italian. Also visit the Forte Montecchio Nord in Colico, one of Europe's most well-preserved fortresses from the First World War.

www.fortedefuentes.it
www.fortemontecchionord.it

Eat
Bellano
Crotto di Biosio
You'll find the restaurant along the Viandante in the hamlet of Biosio above Bellano, although you can also get up there by car. Crotto di Biosio began as Crott del Balin and was a popular stop for those walking the Viandante and for the locals from Bellano to go have a glass of red wine and a bite to eat on a Sunday. The Denti family took over at the beginning of the 1960s, extended the building and opened the Crotto di Biosio. The views of the lake are spectacular.

Crotto di Biosio, Strada di Biosio, www.biosio.it

Lierna
Ristorante il Crotto di Lierna, Lierna
In the village of Lierna, between Mandello del Lario and Lierna, Ristorante il Crotto di Lierna has been here since 1892. It offers typical Lombard cooking which includes lake fish and fresh pasta alongside barbecued meat and fish.

Ristorante il Crotto di Lierna, Via Ducale, 44 www.ristoranteilcrottodilierna.it

Mandello del Lario
Osteria Sali e Tabacchi
Osteria Sali e Tabacchi is in the hamlet of Maggiana above Mandello del Lario and is also along the Viandante. It specialises in local dishes such as freshwater fish. Try

their *taglioni ai missoltini*, fresh taglioni with *missoltini* which are a bit like dried herrings, or their ravioli filled with whitefish which they smoke themselves. They're also renowned for their meat dishes. Try their *coniglio in porchetta* (roasted pork meat) and the *brasato* (stew).

Osteria Sali e Tabacchi, Piazza San Rocco, 3
www.osteriasalietabacchi.it

Stay

Bellano
Fantastica Casa Poppo

Fantastica Casa Poppo is an agriturismo up in Biosio above Bellano right near the Viandante. The agriturismo has its own swimming pool while the accommodation is in individual renovated buildings, each with their own name, and which offer glimpses of spectacular lake views.

Fantastica Casa Poppo, Strada per Biosio,
www.biosio.it

Mandello del Lario
Mamma Ciccia

You'll find Mamma Ciccia in Mandello del Lario. It's a bistro that has both rooms and apartments in a variety of locations throughout the village. It also boasts its own cookery school, so if you're wanting to polish up on your Italian cooking skills while you're here, this is the place.

Mamma Ciccia, Piazza Roma, 15
www.mammaciccia.it

Varenna
Albergo del Sole

Albergo del Sole offers rooms in the main square by the Chiesa di San Giorgio in Varenna. Downstairs there's the pizzeria with tables outside for those early evening aperitivos. It's both central and within easy walking distance of the lake.

Albergo del Sole, Piazza San Giorgio, 17

While You're Here

- Head to Varenna, one of the lake's loveliest villages, and walk along the Passeggiata degli Inammorati (Lovers' Walk). Then sit lakeside and enjoy an aperitivo at one of the bars. www.varennaturismo.it
- Take the number 7 bus from Lecco up to Piani dei Resinelli just below Mount Grignetta and walk to the Parco del Belvedere where you'll find the Passarella Panoramica. It's literally a metal structure which you can walk along to enjoy the views of Lecco and the lake below. Then walk up to Monte Coltignone for views of Resegone and the Valsassina.
- The Orrido di Bellano is the 15-million-year-old natural gorge up in Bellano that you can visit

Varenna. Rachael Martin

Orrido di Bellano. Adobe Stock

along footbridges suspended along the walls. It's also a great day out with children. www.discoveringbellano.eu

- Spend an afternoon at the beach in Abbadia Lariana, always popular with the locals. The campsite Campeggio Spiaggia has both sleep pods and pizza, perfect for after all the walking.
- Colico offers windsurfing, kitesurfing, canoeing and more. You can also hire bikes to explore the Pian di Spagna, just north of Colico, which is famous for its resting and migratory birds. For watersports see www.watersportscenter.it, and www.kitezoo.it who also hire bikes.

Maps, Links and Useful Information

Lecco
www.eccolecco.it offers information in English about the town and lake. Also see www.in-lombardia.it

Viandante
leviedelviandante.eu is the official site for information about all the walks in the area. Also download the app Le Vie del Viandante.

When to go
You can pretty much walk the path all year round, apart from if there's snow in winter. Avoid July and August as it can get very hot and very busy along the lake. Both spring and autumn are perfect, although check in advance for hotels and restaurants as some places do close after the summer season.

Marco / Adobe Stock

VIA FRANCISCA

The Via Francisca links Sorico with Chiavenna, and from then on with the Via Spluga and Switzerland. It's 36km long, and is recommended for seasoned walkers, although of course you don't have to do all of it. At one time it was part of the Antica Via Regina until it was given the name Via Francisca in the thirteenth century, when the routes over the Alps began to be used again. It's thought that its name derives from the French "franchir" which means to travel across or the Latin "franca" which means free, so in this latter sense a free road at a time when many routes were subject to tolls. The walk starts in Sorico at the most northern point of Lake Como where the River Mera comes into the lake. It crosses the natural reserve the Pian di Spagna and the beautiful village of Dascio, which nestles alongside the River Mera. It goes along Lake Mezzola and through various villages until it reaches Gordona, 4.5km outside Chiavenna. From there, it's on to Chiavenna. Don't forget to visit the Collegiate of San Lorenzo when you get there and treat yourself to a typical dinner in a crotto.

For information about the Via Francisca, see **www.leviedelviandante.eu** and the app Le Vie del Viandante.

VIA SPLUGA

When I sit outside the Albergo della Posta up at Montespluga (1,908m) and the Spluga Pass (2,144m), it's here that it always hits me. This is a place that saw merchants, travellers, smugglers, armies and pilgrims go backwards and forwards between Italy and the rest of Europe. It's where the Via Spluga passes through, which together with the system of walks and waterways

Montespluga. Rachael Martin

further south, links Milan to the rest of Europe on the other side of the Alps. The village of Montesplua is still a small collection of houses alongside a couple of hotels, a gift shop and the latteria which sells locally produced cheese. The Via Spluga existed in Roman times when Emperor Augustus decreed that

a road should be built over the pass to go off and conquer the region of Raetia as it was known in Latin. Raetia was the Roman Empire's Alpine province and the Roman's defence against the Germanic peoples often known as the Barbarians.

When the Roman Empire fell in 476, this led to what is now known generally as the Early Middle Ages, previously the Dark Ages. It was a period of instability, wars and immigration of the Germanic peoples. The mountain passes had to be controlled and defended against attack. The eleventh century brought a period of stability and peace and the passes started to open again and become used far more, although it was still quite dangerous to travel through Italy throughout the first half of the twelfth century. Communes or townships were still fighting amongst themselves and in 1167 Frederick Barbarossa conquered Rome.[3] It was the routes across the Alps that played an important part in the development of trade between Northern and Southern Europe. The Alpine regions provided leather, timber, dairy products and animals for slaughter for the cities. The cities gave them iron, clothes and salt.[4] The Via Spluga was one of these routes and highly valued by the Duchy of Milan when they ruled the city during the latter part of the Middle Ages and the Renaissance. It was the main route between Chur in Switzerland and Milan. Later, the postal service came this way on a 36-hour journey from Lindau on Lake Constance to Milan between 1518 and 1826.

When the Austrians took over the Kingdom of Lombardy and Veneto between 1815 to 1866, Francis I, Holy Roman Emperor and Archduke of Austria gave orders for a new road to be built across the pass. This is now the modern road. In this way, they were able to increase trade with the region of Graubünden. Whereas nowadays the modern road closes over the winter, at the time of the Austrians it was kept open.[5] It was also an important source of income for the people of the valley. With the arrival of the railway, other passes such as the Brenner Pass became more important. Later, in 1931, the dam was built. Nowadays the pass is mostly used for tourism purposes, and by those who choose to walk the Via Spluga.

The Via Spluga starts in Thusis in Switzerland and ends at the town of Chiavenna in Valchiavenna, the valley which is named after the town. The walk is 70km long and passes along the Viamala, a series of gorges just after Thusis. From here, it continues to Splügen, a pretty town and characteristic of the area, with its Walser houses. The path then starts to go upwards towards the pass. The view at the top of the pass is impressive, particularly if you look back over the Swiss side with the mountains straight in front of you and the winding road below. When you go over the border you are now in Italy, and below you can see the village of Montespluga.

From Montespluga to Isola

Montespluga for me personally is a place like nowhere else. It's wild, it's remote and it's incredibly beautiful. Leonardo da Vinci mentioned it in his *Codex Atlanticus*, when he spoke of the high and barren mountains up here.[6]

Walking along the Via del Cardinello, Via Spluga. matho / Adobe Stock

Even when you drive up there, there is something so special about seeing the dam and the village of Montespluga at the other end of it.

The most spectacular way of enjoying the Via Spluga is to come down over the Swiss border. You can do it the other way, but coming down has the advantage of giving you those first-class views as you walk. It might not necessarily be easier on the legs, though, as just because you're not walking uphill doesn't mean that it can't be hard work. Spend the night at either the Albergo della Posta or the Albergo Vittoria. Put yourself back in time and imagine you're coming into Italy from Switzerland, sometime in the Middle Ages, heading towards Lake Como and after that Milan.

When you wake up in the morning with all nature's beauty laid out before you, you'll need to take the old route, the one which was used before the Austrians built the road. This route down from Montespluga to Isola is also known as the Via del Cardinello after Monte Cardine, the mountain to the right of the dam as you walk down. It's a spectacular walk that goes down the valley and along the Gola del Cardinello (the gorge of the Cardinello), a mule track which we know was used as far back as 1473.[7] In 1800 General MacDonald, a Marshal of the Napoleonic Empire, brought his troops down this route. It was a disaster, and many troops and animals were lost on the journey. Most of the route is along a mule track, and there are a few places where it is slightly exposed, so be careful if you suffer from vertigo. All in all, it's a fascinating walk along one of Europe's old trade routes. Please note that this is a medium difficulty walk, and usually takes between two and three hours.

When you get to Isola, ideally you"ll have already booked a night at the Locanda Cardinello in advance, which has been a stop for many since 1722. The road continues of course along the river and to Campodolcino, all downhill until you finally reach the elegant town of Chiavenna; the perfect place to relax for a few days after all the walking.

Eat and Stay
Campodolcino
Ristorante La Genzianella
To get there, you'll really need a car, although trust me when I tell you it's worth it. You'll need to go up the hill from Campodolcino to the hamlet of Fraciscio. La Genzianella is pretty much a local institution, and much-loved by many. They have some of the best *pizzoccheri chiavennaschi* you can find in the area, alongside ravioli, meat dishes and the local polenta *taragna*. You will need to book in advance as it gets very busy, especially in summer.

Via Fraciscio, 93, Fraciscio

Isola
Locanda Cardinello

The Locanda Cardinello started life in 1722 as a place for horses to rest on their way down from the Spluga Pass. The Locanda offers rooms and two apartments. The restaurant serves typical dishes from the local area. Look out for the room known as the *stüin* with its old stove and walls completely covered in wood.

Via Baldiscio, 2, Isola di Madesimo, www.locandacardinello.it

Montespluga
Albergo della Posta

Albergo della Posta has been run by the Sala family since the 1950s. We know that Archduke Ranieri of Austria ate here in 1822 in what used to be part of the old customs house. He was the viceroy of the Kingdom of Lombardy and Veneto, which at the time was under Austrian rule, and was here to inaugurate the new road which had been commissioned by Francis I, Holy Roman Emperor and Archduke of Austria. The hotel as we know it today came into life towards the end of the nineteenth century. It has traditionally styled rooms with the option of half board and full board. The restaurant specialises in local dishes from the area and has an *enoteca* which has one of the highest wine cellars in Europe.

Via della Dogana, 8, Madesimo
www.albergopostaspluga.it

Albergo Vittoria Ca' della Montagna

The inn was here as early as 1496 when it offered rest and food to travellers and merchants who were travelling across the pass. It offers seven rooms, two of which are family rooms with four beds. The restaurant serves dishes inspired by the local traditions. You can also order packed lunches and book excursions in the mountains with local guides.

Piazza della Chiesa, 12, Madesimo
www.vittoriamontespluga.com

Ostello Teggiate

Ostello Teggiate opened in 2023 in the building where horses were changed in summer and sledges repaired in winter. It then became a *casa cantoniera*, the place in the mountains which is responsible for the maintenance of a section of road, usually about 3km or 4km long, and for the onward progress of goods and post. It's still the original red colour of the *casa cantoniera*, is situated on the side of the road as you go up to Montespluga and has stunning views across the valley. The hostel offers various rooms and a menu which changes daily in the restaurant. The bar is the place where the horses were kept, which really gives a feeling of its history.

SS 36 del Lago di Como e dello Spluga, 14, Madesimo
www.ostelloteggiate.it

Chiavenna, Leonardo da Vinci and the Crotti

We know that Leonardo da Vinci went to Chiavenna and the Valchiavenna Valley many times when he lived at the court of Ludovico the moor in Milan. Da Vinci loved to study water and knew both the *crotti* and the River Mera and the waterfall known as the Cascate dell'Acqua Fraggia, all of which he wrote about it in the *Codex Atlanticus*. The *crotti*, an old term for grottoes, are literally natural fridges. They were made possible because of a constant current of air known as the *sòrel* which comes out of the mountain. Gradually over the years, families added buildings around them. Families often had their own *crotto* where they would go up on feast days and eat and drink with friends. If passers-by were in the area, they too were welcome. Some of these *crotti* were used as trattorias as far back as the fifteenth century when Da Vinci visited.[8] They offered cured meats, cheese and wine, and then in the 20th century some of them became proper trattorias, and other typical dishes from the area were added to the menu. The *pizzoccheri chiavennaschi* are particular to this valley. They're a type of roughly shaped *gnocchi* made with flour which are cooked and then mixed with butter and cheese. The typical *crotto* menu also includes grilled meats and polenta, and potatoes cooked on a *piota*, a special type of stone which is used for cooking. Don't forget to try the *biscotti di Prosto*, the local biscuits. They're crumbly, buttery and delicious. The Sagra dei Crotti is the annual festival of the crotti that takes place during the first two weeks of September. You do need to book tickets for it in

Chiavenna. Rachael Martin

advance. See www.sagradeicrotti.it for details. If you'd like to eat at one of the local *crotti,* try the Crotto del Prato or Crotto Ombra in town along the Pratogiano, which is the area of the *crotti* in town. Slightly further out you'll find the Crotto Quartino in Piuro, near the Cascate di Acquafraggia.

www.crottodelprato.it
www.crottoombra.com
crottoquartino.it

While You're Here

- Madesimo is the local ski resort that is popular with the Milanese, some of whom have second homes here. In summer, apart from the central weeks of August, it's a quiet resort, and a great base from which to explore the area. It's known for its huge statue of the Madonna d'Europa up on the mountain above the town. The town is also associated with Italian poet and writer Giosuè Carducci, who spent many summers here. There are plenty of walks leading out of the town up to the surrounding mountains and to the Spluga Pass. Note that there is a regular free bus service between Montespluga, Isola, Campodolcino and Chiavenna in summer, which makes it easier to get around. For information about walks in Madesimo, see **madesimo.eu** and **www.madesimo.com**.
- The Parco delle Marmitte dei Giganti in Chiavenna, roughly translated as the Park of the Giants' Pans, has been a natural reserve since 1996. It's renowned for its rock formations and pools of water formed from glaciers. The whole walk takes about an hour and a half. See **valchiavenna.com** for details.
- Visit the hamlet of Fraciscio above Campodolcino and walk down to the river and along to Gualdera, a lovely mountain plain where you

Madesimo. Rachael Martin

Gualdera. Rachael Martin

can grab a coffee at Albergo La Montanina. They also do amazing cakes and have deck chairs to hire. Continue across and upwards to the village of Bondeno.

- Go up the Calvario to the Alpe Angeloga. Do be aware that it's a steep walk which involves going up rocks with an altitude difference of 600m. The walk starts as you come out of Fraciscio higher up, where you can park your car if you have one. You then go up for around two hours, depending on how quickly you take it, to the Rifugio Chiavenna up at 2,044m. The mountain above is Pizzo Stella (3,163m), the valley's most famous peak which was first climbed by English mountaineer John Ball in in 1865. It is not an easy mountain walk by any means, but so worth it when you get there.
- For food and other goodies, head to the Pratogiano Market which is held in Chiavenna every Saturday morning. Don't forget to stop for coffee at Pasticceria Mastai. www.mastai.it

Maps, Links and Useful Information
Valchiavenna
www.valchiavenna.com is the website of the tourism association Consorzio Promozione Turistica Valchiavenna, and has plenty of ideas for what to do in the area.

www.valtellina.it also has information about Chiavenna and the surrounding area.

Via Spluga
viaspluga.com provides maps and information about the Via Spluga.

See leviedelviandante.eu and the Le Vie del Viandante app for maps and information regarding the Via Spluga and walks which link the Valle dello Spluga with Val Mescolina.

When to go
The best time to walk the Via Spluga is in late spring, summer or early autumn, although the last stretch to Chiavenna can be hot in summer as Chiavenna is at a lower altitude. The pass closes during winter because of the snow.

GETTING HERE AND GETTING AROUND

Fly to one of the Milan airports: Malpensa, Linate or Orio al Serio. Malpensa has direct trains to both Milan and Como. From Linate, take the metro M4. Trains to Milan, Como, Lecco go from the Centrale and Garibaldi stations. Orio al Serio airport is near Bergamo, where you can get a direct train to Lecco. Trains go straight up from Lecco along the lake to Colico and then on to Chiavenna. For the Via Antica Regina, get a train to Como and then get the bus or boat if you're starting further up. Boats also leave from Varenna to Menaggio or Cernobbio.

3

EMILIA-ROMAGNA

→ Via Romea Germanica – Stade to Rome
 • Polesella to Ferrara
→ Via degli Dei / Way of the Gods – Bologna to Florence (Tuscany)
→ Via della Lana e della Seta / The Wool and Silk Road – Bologna to Prato (Tuscany)
→ Via Mater Dei – Bologna to Riola

INTRODUCTION

Emilia-Romagna is made up of two areas; Emilia in the west and Romagna in the east, which are joined by the Roman road, the Via Emilia. This ancient road went from Piacenza in the west to Rimini on the west coast. It was around 230km long and was built in 187 BC by Marcus Aemilius Lepidus, from whom it takes its name. He built it to quickly transfer troops backwards and forwards from Rimini. The Romans had just conquered the Gauls in Bologna, while Piacenza was still surrounded by Gauls and so it was vital to be able to move the troops fast to suppress them.[1] Nowadays the Via Emilia is the main road which links Emilia and Romagna and goes through the area known as the region's Motor Valley. Think Ferrari in Maranello, Maserati and Pagani in Modena, and Ducati and Lamborghini in Bologna. It really is a petrolhead's dream, and if that weren't enough, there's the annual Gran Prix at the Enzo and Dino Ferrari racetrack in Imola.

In the far east of the region is the 120km long Riviera Romagnola. It's one of the most popular Italian coasts for families, while the resort of Rimini is a rite of passage for many an Italian teenager. Bologna is the region's capital, often known in Italian as *la dotta, la grassa, la rossa*, translated as 'the learned, the fat and the red'. It's 'learned' because of its university, founded in 1088 and said to be the oldest university in the world which

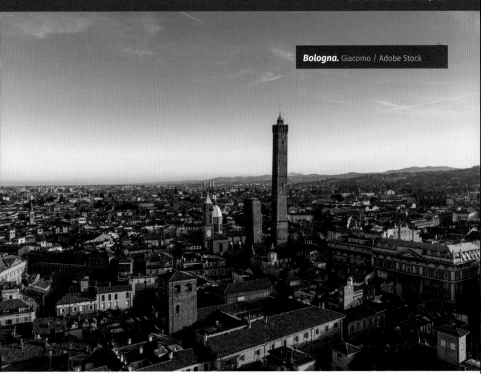

Bologna. Giacomo / Adobe Stock

Modena. ClickAlps / Adobe Stock

is still open today. It's 'fat' because of its food, while 'red' comes from the bricks from which its buildings are built, and also because historically, after the Second World War, Bologna always veered politically to the left. It's sometimes called Bologna la turrita or Bologna 'the turreted', in reference to its many towers which were built over the years by the most important families of the city. The Torre degli Asinelli (Tower of the Donkeys) is the city's symbol.

The landscape in Emilia-Romagna is varied. The north is flat while the south is hilly and mountainous, and part of the Appenine mountain range which runs all the way down Italy. Monte Cimone is the highest mountain in Emilia-Romagna at 2,165m. There are various walks that go over the Appenines and join Emilia-Romagna with Tuscany. The Regional Park of the Po Delta in the east is an area of beauty which is all its own, and a fascinating area to explore. It's also within visiting distance of Venice and the charming seaside town of Chioggia, its own type of mini-Venice on water. Ravenna and Ferrara are also nearby. It's here at the River Po in the village of Polesella that we'll join the Via Romea Germanica. These are flat walks which can be taken at leisure as you enjoy the surrounding landscape.

LOCAL FOOD

When in Emilia-Romagna, eat. When in Italy eat, but really, Emilia-Romagna is a pasta-lover's paradise. It includes fresh hand-rolled pasta such as *lasagne* and *tortellini*, but also *tagliatelle, garganelli, fettuccine, tortellini, anolini, cappellacci* and *cappelletti*. This is a culinary build-your-own memories of that particular trattoria in that particular town. Also look out for *tigelle*, small focaccia which are often filled with local *salumi* or cold meats. Then there's *gnocco fritto*, a mix of flour, water, lard and milk which is fried and again served

with *salumi*. *Parmiggiano Reggiano* (parmesan cheese) is made in Parma, along with *Prosciutto di Parma* (Parma ham) and *Culatello di Zibello*, another type of cured ham which has DOP (protected designation of origin) status. *Zampone* and *cotechino* are both cured meats which are cooked. *Cotechino* is often eaten on New Year's Eve with lentils. Street food in Romagna includes the popular piadina. It's a type of flatbread which is filled, folded and warmed, often with Parma ham, rocket and *stracchino* cheese. The area around Ravenna and along the coast is known

Tortellini al ragù. jimenezar / Adobe Stock

for its fish. Fried or grilled eel is a local speciality, as is frog soup, duck in honey, and lamb. Polenta with clams or *vongole* is also popular, as is *coniglio in porchetta alla romognola* (rabbit covered in porchetta).

VIA ROMEA GERMANICA

The Via Romea Germanica starts in Lower Saxony in the north of Germany, and just as its name would imply, leads to Rome. Albert of Stade was a Benedictine monk, born at the end of the twelfth century, who became abbot at the Benectine monastery of Saint Mary of Stade in 1232. Albert didn't like what he considered the relaxed rules at the monastery and wanted to change it to the Cistercian Order, but to do this he had to gain permission from Pope Gregory IX. So he set off to Rome to see the Pope. The Pope gave him permission, but when he got back home, the local powers refused the change. So in 1240 he left the Benedictine Order and went to join the Franciscan monks and live by their vow of poverty.

Around the time of his journey to Rome, Albert had started to write his Latin chronicle *Annales Stadenses*, the *Annals of Stade*. Annals were medieval documents in which events were recorded year by year. Albert's *Annals* start at the Creation and go up to the year 1256.[2] It was in these annals that he documented his journey to Rome via a conversation between monks in which they discuss the best way to get to Rome. Making the journey to Rome as a medieval monk was extremely important. For those who couldn't, they would often create pilgrimages at home where they would walk the same number of kilometres as an act of devotion.[3] At the time there were three major routes which led across Europe: the Via Francigena, which led from Canterbury and through France and Switzerland into Italy; the Via Romea Germanica; and what we now call the Via Romea Strata, which is really a collection of various pilgrimage routes and Roman roads all leading to Rome. It became the Via Romea Strata in 2015 when Raimondo Sinibaldi decided to bring them all together and make one route.[4] These roads which make up the Via Romea Strata brought pilgrims to Rome from Eastern Europe. What we

Euganean hills. davide / Adobe Stock

know as the Via Romea Strata today starts in Tallinn in Estonia and goes through Latvia, Lithuania, Poland, the Czech Republic and into Austria, where it enters Italy over the Passo del Tarvisio into Friuli-Venezia Giulia. The route the Via Romea Germanica follows today is according to Albert's *Annals*, which are now at the library in Wolfenbüttel in Germany. In 2007, when Giovanni Caselli started a project to bring the walk back to life, he used this document. In 2010, and later in 2013, signs were put up to mark sections of the route.[5] This is the same Giovanni Caselli who researched the Via Francigena in the 1980s and walked it himself to trace and document it all.

The entire route from Stade to Rome is 2,200km long, crosses through three countries and has ninety-seven stages.

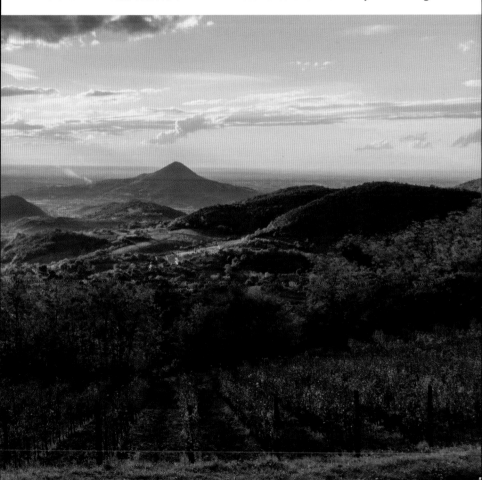

It's the route that was used not only by those travelling from Germany, but also by people travelling from Scandinavia, Poland and the Baltic regions. From Stade it goes through Germany via the states of Thüringen and Bavaria, into Italy and on to Rome. It comes into Italy at the Brenner Pass in the Alpine region of Trentino-Alto Adige and the spectacular landscapes of the Dolomite mountains, where it makes its way through Vipiteno, Bressanone, Bolzano and Trento. It then goes into the region of Veneto, along the Brenta River, to Padua and finally to the Colli Euganei or Euganean hills. They're named after the ancient population the *Euganei* who lived here. If they look somewhat like volcanoes, it's because they're ancient extinct volcanoes. From here, the route continues through Emilia-Romagna, Umbria and Tuscany and Tuscia, the area which was once home of the Etruscan people. The next stop is Rome and Saint Peter's Square.

From Polesella to Ferrara and Beyond

The beauty of walking this section of the way is that it gives you the opportunity to see both Ferrara and the countryside out towards the Valli di Camacchio. It's flat walking before it goes towards Tuscany up the mountain pass Passo Serra and over the Appenine Mountains. The first section of our walk is from Polesella to Ferrara, a 22.5-km long flat walk. This is walking out in the countryside which presents no particular difficulties. Polesella is a small village in the province of Rovigo in

Casal Borsetti. francescodemarco Adobe Stock

Ferrara

For any pilgrim, and for any pilgrim or walker today, arriving in Ferrara was a major event. Obizzo d'Este of the powerful Este family took over the city in 1264, and for the next three hundred years Ferrara flourished under the House of Este. In 1492 architect Biagio Rossetti planned the city to include all its main buildings, with wide streets, gardens, quiet squares; everything that a Renaissance city would require. It was the ideal city and was admired throughout Europe. The Este family were also responsible for commissioning a wealth of artistic treasures. Between the fifteenth and sixteenth centuries, Piero della Francesca, Andrea Mantegna and Jacopo Bellini all came here to develop the Este palaces. The Este dukes also developed the Po Delta, with canals, villages and beautiful villas known as *Delizie Estensi*. It's a pleasure to explore and it's no surprise that the city has been a UNESCO World Heritage site since 1995. Visit the Castello Estense, the castle built by the Este family in 1385. Lucrezia Borgia lived here with her husband Alfonso I Este, Duke of Ferrara. Also visit the city's cathedral, the Cattedrale di San Giorgio. It's the city's most important church that was built from the twelfth century onwards. It's in Piazza delle Erbe, the town's main square along with other important monuments such as Palazzo della Ragione and the Loggia dei Merciai. The first was the old courthouse – literally translated it means the Palace of Reason – while the second used to be the textiles market.

For more information about Ferrara, visit www.ferraraterraeacqua.it

Castello Estense, Ferrara.
Adobe Stock / Leonid Andronov

Valli di Comacchio

The Po Delta Park is the largest brackish wetlands in Italy, and one of the most important in Europe. The Valli di Comacchio is the lagoon inside it that covers 11,000 acres. The area is a paradise for nature lovers, and home to many types of animals and vegetation, including the famous pink flamingoes which make their appearance between spring and late summer. The Valli di Comacchio is also known for fishing, and in particular eel fishing, and for the Salina di Comacchio, the salt flats where the flamingoes gather. The town of Comacchio, often known as "Little Venice" with its famous seventeenth-century Trepponti Bridge is definitely worth a visit. Don't miss the fish market known as Mercato Ittico at Porto Garibaldi and take a boat trip along the canal.

www.visitcomacchio.it/en/what-to-do/trekking has details of local walks.

Also see www.podeltatourism.it/en/il-delta-del-po/comacchio-s-lagoons

Valli di Comacchio. Maurizio Sartoretto / Adobe Stock

Veneto along the Po Delta, and known for its seventeenth century Villa Ca' Rosetta. The walk takes you along the River Po, until you then leave it behind you to go towards Ferrara. You get to Ferrara through the sixteenth century Porta degli Angeli. Medieval Ferrara had its own Porta degli Pellegrini (Gate of the Pilgrims) which pilgrims always passed through on their way to Rome. It was at the end of Via San Romano, one of the city's most important streets, and was eventually dismantled in the eighteenth century. Go see the medieval cathedral Cattedrale di San Giorgio Martire. It was inaugurated in 1135, and an essential stop for all medieval pilgrims. Pope Urban III was buried here in 1187.

From Ferrara, you then go out along the canals to the hamlet of Traghetto in Argenta. The Pieve di San Giorgio in Argenta is one of the oldest churches in Emilia-Romagna and dates from 569. From Argenta, it's onwards to the Valli di Camacchio. Casalborsetti is a small coastal resort in the province of Ravenna on the Adriatic Sea. This all covers four stages of the walk, which aren't particularly difficult, if long. They offer wonderful views of the countryside and the marshlands of the Valli di Camacchio. You could stay in the area and choose several stages interspersed with local sightseeing. When the walk arrives in Casalborsetti, you're now just over 500km from Rome.

Eat

Comacchio
Locanda La Comacina,
Locanda La Comacina is along the canals, and is renowned for its pasta dishes and barbecued local fish. They also have rooms.

Via Edgardo Fogli, 17-19
www.lacomacina.it

Ferrara
Cusina e Butega
Situated near the Chiesa di San Paolo, Cusina e Butega offer local dishes and wine. Try their *cappellacci alla zucca* (pasta filled with butternut squash).

Corso Porta Reno, 28
www.cusinaebutega.com

Osteria La Compagnia
Set in a typical *cassero ferrarese*, the country houses you find here, this welcoming osteria serves typical dishes made with local products, and homemade pastas such as *cappellacci* served with ragù or butter and sage.

Piazza Sacrati, 32
www.osterialacompagnia.it

Stay

Francolino
Delizia d'Este
Delizia d'Este is an agriturismo just outside Ferrara in the village of Francolino near the River Po. It's in

the Parco Urbano, where the Este hunting grounds used to be. The accommodation is bed and breakfast in a typical cottage, and they have single, double and triple rooms, all named after members of the Este family.

Via Calzolai, 259, Ferrara
www.deliziadeste.it

Ferrara
D'Elite Room and Breakfast
This charming bed and breakfast in the historical centre of Ferrara is within easy walking distance of the main sights. Please note that some of the rooms are in a separate building.

Via Francesco del Rossa, 9
www.delite.it

Maxxim Hotel
Set in the beautiful Palazzo Beccari-Freguglia in the historical centre, the hotel has original features and two inner courtyards for breakfast.

Via Ripagrande, 21
www.maxxim.it

Maps, Links and Useful Information
Emilia-Romagna
www.emiliaromagnaturismo.it
www.travelemiliaromagna.it and emiliaromagnawelcome.com all have information about the region. See www.camminiemiliaromagna.it for maps, itineraries and information about walks.

Via Romea Germanica
The official website is viaromeagermanica.com with maps, itineraries and and useful information. Also see www.camminiemiliaromagna.it

When to go
As always, summer can get very hot for walking, so spring and autumn are better times of year to visit.

While You're Here
- Visit the Delizie Estensi, the country estates of the Este family, with their agricultural estates and large gardens. They're just outside Ferrara in the Po Delta, which the Este dukes developed. They built canals, roads, and these beautiful Renaissance villas.
- Continue the Via Romea Germanica from Casalborsetti to nearby Ravenna and swoon over the Byzantine mosaics, a legacy of when Ravenna was part of the Byzantine Empire during the 5th and 6th centuries. They're said to be some of the most beautiful in the world and are spread throughout the town's eight early Christian monuments, all of which are now UNESCO sites. The town is also famous for its links with Italian poet Dante Alighieri, who wrote The Divine Comedy which he finished in 1302. Dante is considered the father of the Italian language because he was

The sixth century apse mosaic at San Vitale, Ravenna. pfeifferv / Adobe Stock

Comacchio. dvoevnone / Adobe Stock

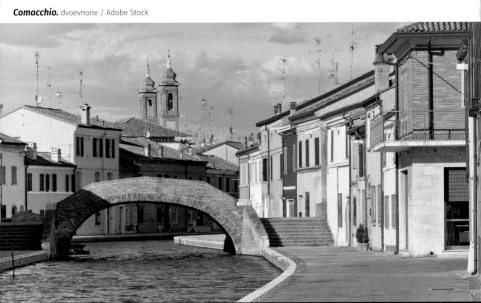

the first writer to create a literary work out of spoken language. At the time Latin was considered the language of learning. www.ravennamosaici.it

- Visit the Museo Delta Antico in Comacchio. Through over 2,000 finds, it explains the history of the Po Delta from classical times to today. www.museodeltaantico.com
- Take the boat from the Pesca Foce fishing station in the Po Delta Park to see the old fishing houses and enjoy the natural landscapes that surround you. For details, see the section Boat Trips at www.podeltatourism.it
- Spend a day at the beach at Marina di Ravenna. What grew up as a fishing village between the nineteenth and twentieth centuries is now a pleasant resort with a long sandy beach surrounded by pine woods.

WALKS ACROSS THE APPENINES

The following walks link Emilia-Romagna with Tuscany, apart from Via Mater Dei which is all in Emilia-Romagna. The walks go over or into the Appenine Mountains and because of this are for experienced walkers. Obviously, you don't have to do a whole walk but can pick and choose as you please. What matters is that you get out there, start walking and enjoy what you see, or alternatively, that you are inspired to enjoy the views from the comfort of your home. For this reason, I have included plenty of links to give a good idea of the area and the walks involved.

Via degli Dei / Way of the Gods

The Via degli Dei or Way of the Gods starts and finishes in two of the most beautiful piazzas in two of the most beautiful cities of art in Italy. The first, where the walk starts, is Piazza Maggiore in Bologna, one of the largest squares in Europe, and the heart of Bologna. It dates from 1200 but wasn't known as Piazza Maggiore until the sixteenth century. The second is Piazza della Signoria in Florence, the main square in the city that is known as the cradle of the Renaissance. In between there are the Tuscan-Emilian Appenines. The walk is 130km long and is of medium difficulty. Of course, you don't have to do any of the actual stages as such. You can also pick and choose and visit a few relevant places and take a walk along the path as you please.

The walk is called the Way of the Gods because it passes over four mountains which take their names from Roman gods and goddesses: Monte Adone (Mount Adonis), Monte Luario (Mount Luna), Monzuno from Monte di Giove (Mount Jupiter), and Monte Venere (Mount Venus). It offers

Rock formations on Monte Adone.
alessio / Adobe Stock

View of Florence from Fiesole.
eddygaleotti / Adobe Stock

fantastic views of the mountains and countryside, has a rich cultural heritage and a fascinating history. Historians believe that the route was initially used by the Etruscans. They lived in an area known as Etruria in what is now Tuscany, Lazio and northern Umbria for several hundred years, before the Romans took control at the end of the fourth century BC. After this, a road was built by the Roman consul Gaius Flaminius in 187 BC. It went along the same route but was longer as this new road linked Bologna with Arezzo, south of Florence. It was built to make it easier to transfer troops across the Appenine Mountains, and so they used the Etruscan path. Over time, the Roman road became hidden, but we know that it was still much used by travellers during the Middle Ages as it was the most direct route over the Appenines.

The Via degli Dei falls into a group of walks which were developed at the beginning of the 1990s, often inspired by ancient routes that are brought together to make a single one for walkers and tourists. Part of it follows the same route as the Via Flaminia Militare, also known as the Via Flaminia Minor. In fact, you can still see what remains of the Via Flaminia Militare along it. What matters is that you walk,[6]

Linea Gotica / The Gothic Line

Firenzuola was at the heart of the Gothic Line created by the Germans during the Second World War to hold out against the Allies who were moving up from the south. The village was bombed and destroyed on 12 September 1944. Nowadays there is a museum, the Museo Storico Etnografico e della Linea Gotica, which explores the history behind it. During the Second World War the Appenine Mountains saw fierce fighting and some of the most tragic events in recent Italian history. The Allies had landed in Sicily on 9 July 1943, bombed Rome shortly after, and Mussolini was removed on 25 July. On 3 September an armistice was secretly signed with the Allies, which was announced publicly on 8 September. Germany entered northern Italy and occupied it, supported by the Italian fascists. The Gothic Line was the German response. It was a line of defence which ran from just above Ravenna near the Valli di Comacchio, literally, the fish basins of Comacchio, to Massa Carrrara above Viareggio in Tuscany to the west. All along the line fighting took place as the Germans tried to hold their defence and the Allies and Italian Partisans tried to push forward. Local people were often involved, and they frequently took enormous risks. Raids and round ups were common such as in Sant'Anna di Stazzema and Marrzabotto. The fighting went on for 20 months until 25 April 1945 when Mussolini was captured and killed. Nowadays you can walk along the Gothic Line which has been retraced by Vito Paticchia, a long-time member of the Club Alpino Italiano and an expert in trails across the mountains.

For further information about the Cammino della Linea Gotica (Way of the Gothic Line) see www.lineagotica.eu.

and whether this is the exact same route that medieval travellers or Roman soldiers took, it still speaks the history of such times.

So where does it take you? You go out of Bologna and reach the village of Badolo. Bear in mind that this is a walk of over 20km which goes up and down with significant differences in altitude, so you might want to study the maps first and select sections. All links can be found at the end of this chapter. Badolo is famous for its Rocca di Badolo, a huge rock face that is now popular with climbers, and where findings have been made relating to the Bronze Age. There's also a very nice restaurant with views across the countryside, Antica Hostaria Rocca di Badolo if you fancy just going up there and taking a walk. The route then passes through sites of historical interest such as the Madonna dei Fornelli sanctuary, literally Madonna of the little ovens. The name comes from the way in which the monks used to make charcoal from wood to keep warm during the cold winter months. Further on, Firenzuola is on the Emilian-Tuscan border in the area known as the Mugello. It's sometimes known as a *terra di mezzo* or middle earth. Its origins date back to Roman times when the Via Flaminia Miilitare was being built. The town we see today was founded in 1350 by the Medici family of Florence, who according to legend and literary texts from the time, came from the Mugello. This is an area of wild borderlands, scattered with historical villages and medieval castles and churches, and this is where its fascination lies. The last village before Florence is Fiesole. Take a slight detour up Montefiesole for the best view of Florence in the distance. Florence is where the Renaissance was born and here you have it all in front of you. It's certainly a feast for the eyes.

Via Della Lana e Della Seta / The Wool and Silk Road

The Wool and Silk road links Bologna with the city of Prato which lies 38km north-west of Florence. During the Middle Ages, Prato and the whole Florentine area had started to become

La Rupe / The Rock, Sasso Marconi.
luciap / Adobe Stock

famous for wool and silk, although the story goes back further. In 540 the city of Ravenna, known as Classe after the Roman *classis* or fleet, was taken by the Byzantines and became part of the Byzantine Empire. Ravenna had links with the Silk Roads in the east. Bologna is about 80km from Ravenna and silk production began there as early as the sixth century. It was from around the fifteenth century onwards that Bologna really became famous for its silkworms and silk production as it had a system of canals which enabled it to develop

silk mills. Thanks to these mills and advanced production techniques, the city gained a reputation for silk production all over the known world. Prato also had a system of canals, which enabled them to build mills. In Prato, the people became well-known for their weaving skills, both of wool and silk, which were an art form and a powerful source of trade and income. Weaving wasn't just confined to Prato but to the whole area around Florence. The Wool and Silk Road was therefore a way for merchants to come backwards and forwards over the Appenine Mountains, and this is why the route now carries this name. While silk production in Bologna lasted until the eighteenth century, Prato is still famous for its textile industries today. Many fashion houses still head there to get their fabrics from Prato.

The route you follow today is a very recent invention. The idea belonged to Vito Paticchia, who also traced the Cammino della Linea Gotica (Way of the Gothic Line). The walk was inaugurated in June 2018. Just like the Via degli Dei, it's a form of slower tourism that allows you to get closer to the history and culture of an area, and to learn so much that you might not necessarily have come across if you hadn't just started to put one foot in front of the other and walk. The way is 139km long and is spilt into six stages, so six stages for six days if you want to think of it like that. Do be aware that this is quite a demanding walk of between 20km to 30km each day, with significant differences in altitude. Like all the walks over the Appenines, these are not exactly Sunday strolls. The starting point is Bologna, in Piazza Maggiore. This is the easiest stretch of the walk as the difference in altitude is much less. Basically, you go up 230m and down 200m, which is a lot different to going up an altitude difference of 1,400m!

Most of the route is flat and it's a very pleasant and enjoyable walk along the canal. As you go, look out for the portcullis or *grada* along Via della Grada, which also illustrates how the canal was also used as a system of defence. At Casalecchio di Reno, there's the Chiusa di Casalecchio or Lock of Casalecchio, which was awarded UNESCO status in 2015. Its origins date back to the end of the twelfth century and it's the oldest hydraulic structure in Europe which still works and is still in continuous use today. It monitors the flow of the river into the city by sending part of the water into the Canale di Reno (Reno Canal). It's this that enabled Bologna's silk production industry by providing the mills and factories with water, all of which in turn played a large part in contributing to the city's wealth. The walk then continues to Sasso Marconi, just before you start to climb up into the hills and mountains. The walk to Sasso Marconi takes six hours, while the walk to Casalecchio di Reno is 6km.

Via Mater Dei

Via Mater Dei, Latin for Way of the Mother of God, is another beautiful walk across the Appenine Mountains, which takes you to ten sanctuaries all dedicated to the Virgin Mary. The walk is essentially a pilgrimage and provides the opportunity for prayer and reflection along the way. The idea is that as you walk, you are walking towards and getting closer to the Virgin Mary. Of course, it doesn't have to be a pilgrimage, but for me personally there is always something about visiting sanctuaries in natural surroundings which prompts reflection, whether you believe or not.

The route starts in the Santuario di Santa Maria della Vita in the Quadrilatero area of Bologna. Whereas Milan's quadrilatero is all about the fashion, in Bologna it's all about the food. It's a lively area in the centre which is great for individual food shops known as *botteghe*. They include fishmongers, butchers, and fresh fruit and vegetable shops, alongside restaurants and cafés. The area started life in the Middle Ages. It was where the people of the city used to gather, eat or go shopping, very much like today. It's the perfect place to have a cappuccino and a brioche before you set off. It's also home to the city's oldest osteria, Osteria del Sole, which opened in 1465. Go there today and you'll still find long tables along which everyone sits, just

Santuario delle Madonna di San Luca. Frank Krautschick / Adobe Stock

like it used to be in the past. Please note that the osteria only serves beer and wine so if you want to eat, you can buy something from the surrounding shops and take it in with you. For food, head to Osteria Bottega.

Now that we've dealt with the essentials, the Santuario di Santa Maria della Vita here is a twelfth sanctuary dedicated to the Virgin Mary in the local Baroque style. It's famous for its *Compianto sul Cristo Morto* (Lamentation over the Dead Christ) by Niccolò dell'Arca, a group of seven life-size figures sculpted from terracotta and dated 1463. The walk then takes you under the San Luca portico, the longest in the world, and which also has UNESCO status. It leads up the hill known as the Colle della Guardia to where you'll find the next sanctuary, the twelfth century Santuario della Madonna di San Luca. It's after this that you start to leave Bologna and head for Val di Zena before going up into the Appenines. From here you go from one sanctuary to another, a walk of shrines, sanctuaries, villages and castles, each with their own story to tell. The walk is 157km long, has eight stages and offers stunning views of the surrounding countryside. Highlights include the beautifully conserved villages of La Scola, Sterpi and Qualto, and the eighteenth century sanctuary, the Madonna dei Boschi, which is looked after by the friars. They arrived here in 2013 and brought a daily mass

at 7am, and at 9am on Sundays. The shrine to the Mater Pacis or Mother of Peace up on Monte Calvo was placed there in 2020 in the heartland of the Linea Gotica. It's a sobering reminder of what people in these mountains lived through. The walk ends in Riolo but before you get there, there's the Santuario della Beata Vergine della Consolazione on Mount Montovolo. In Etruscan times there was a temple to the Goddess Pale. Now there's a Romanic church dated 1211. Your final destination is the Church of Santa Maria Assunta in Riola di Vergato. It's a modern church which was designed by the Norwegian architect, Alvar Aalto. He came to the site in 1966, noticed there was no church, and thought it would make a perfect position near the river and the village. Building started in 1976 and the church was inaugurated in 1978.

Eat in Bologna

Ristorante da Bertino
Alberto Roda, known as Bertino, started the restaurant back in 1957. Today it's run by his son and daughter, Stefano and Claudia. It serves local dishes of fresh pasta, meat, and delicious desserts.

Via delle Lame, 55
www.ristorantedabertino.it

Trattoria del Biassanot
Look out for the sign with the black cat under the portico. Trattoria

del Biassanot specialises in homemade fresh pasta. Also try their antipasto with the local cold meats, accompanied by a glass of local Lambrusco wine.

Via Piella, 16/A
www.dalbiassanot.it

Trattoria Zita
Try the *bollito al carrello* or their *arrosto al carrello*. *Bollito al carrello* is a selection of various meats including the local *cotechino, zampone* and *testina* (part of the head), while the *arrosto* version includes local roast ham *Prosciutto di Praga* and *capocollo*, also known as *coppa*.

Via Emilia Ponente, 68
www.trattoriazita.it

The following are in the Quadrilatero:

Osteria del Sole
Vicolo Ranocchi, 1/d, Bologna
www.osteriadelsole.it

Osteria Bottega
Via Santa Caterina, 51, Bologna

Stay in Bologna
Casa Bertagni
Boutique guest house in the historical centre near the university, within walking distance of all the major sites of interest.

Via Giovanni Battista de Rolandis, 7
www.casabertagni.it

Good Morning Bologna
Good Morning Marsala and Good Morning 'Al Teatro' are two central hotels are both in the historical centre of Bologna. One is on Via Marsala and the other is near the Teatro Comunale.

Via Marsala, 20/2 and Via delle Bellearti, 16
www.goodmorningbologna.com

Eat and Stay Along the Via degli Dei / Way of the Gods
Antica Hostaria della Rocca di Badolo, Badolo
Typical osteria in Rocca di Badolo which specialises in local dishes using seasonal produce such as truffle, wild mushrooms and game.

Via Brento, 4, Badolo
www.hostariadibadolo.it

Vecchia Trattoria Monte Adone, Monzuno
Serves traditional Bolognese and Emilian dishes, including fresh pasta dressed in a variety of ways and local meat dishes.

Via Castellazzo, 4, Monzuno
www.trattoriamonteadone.it

Eat and Stay Along the Via della Lana e della Seta / Wool and Silk Road
Locanda 3 Virtù, Sasso Marconi
The locanda has been open for business since the early twentieth century. It offers local dishes alongside those with an innovative touch, and has a well

stocked selection of wine. They have single, double, triple and quadruple rooms and a small apartment. Please note that the Wool and Silk Road also passes through Sasso Marconi.

Via Ponte Albano, 97, Sasso Marconi
www.locanda3virtu.it

Albergo Bar Ristorante Il Ponte, Castiglione dei Pepoli

This bar, restaurant and hotel has been run by the Mattei family since the beginning of the twentieth century. The restaurant offers local cooking, while the hotel has simple and quiet single, double, triple and quadruple rooms.

Via G. Pepoli, 32, Castiglione dei Pepoli
www.albergo-ilponte.it

Eat and Stay Along the Via Mater Dei
Albergo Ristorante Poli, Madonna dei Fornelli

Home cooked local dishes and double and single rooms. They also offer half board and full board options.

Locanda del Pellegrino, Baragazza

Traditional inn which offers local home cooking and rooms.

Via Bocca di Rio, 20, Baragazza
www.locandadelpellegrino.business.site

Maps, Links and Useful Information
Emilia-Romagna

The official tourist site of the region is www.emiliaromagnaturismo.it and has plenty of useful information for your visit. Also see www.emiliaromagnawelcome.com and www.travelemiliaromagna.it.

Bologna

Both www.welcomebologna.com and www.bologna-guide.com have information about what to see and do in Bologna. For more information about Bologna's system of canals, see canalidibologna.it

Walks in Emilia-Romagna

For information about the area, visit www.camminiemiliaromagna.it and www.travelemiliaromagna.it

Via degli Dei / Way of the Gods

For information and maps, visit www.viadeglidei.it

Via della Lana e della Seta / Wool and Silk Road

For information and maps, visit www.viadellalanaedellaseta.it

Via Mater Dei

For information and maps, visit www.materdei.it

Guides

See www.appeninoslow.it for organised tours.

When to go

The best time to visit would be spring, late summer and early autumn.

Summers can be very hot for walking, while winters can be very cold with snow.

While You're Here

- Spend the day in Bologna and take in the sights. Start in Piazza Maggiore with coffee outside one of the cafés. Visit the Torre degli Asinelli, visit the Basilica di San Petronio and walk under the city's porticoes. Don't forget a trip to the city's food area known as the Quadrilatero, which dates back to the Middle Ages, or the Mercato di Mezzo, also from the same period.
- Visit the Museo del Tessuto in Prato, the textiles museum which explores the history of textiles and weaving in the city from the Middle Ages to the current day. The town has various parks to walk in and explore such as Parco delle Cascine di Tavola, Parco di Galceti and Villa Medicea di Poggia in Caiano. **www.museodeltessuto.it**
- Visit the Palazzo Ducale in Sassuolo and take a walk in the gardens there. Francesco I d'Este took an old castle and transformed into a beautiful country residence known as a *delizia* or delight. **www.visitmodena.it**
- Spend a day at the Parco dei Gessi Bolognesi e Calanchi dell'Abbadessa (Bolognese Gypsum and the Abbadessa

Palazzo Ducale, Sassuolo. ginettigino / Adobe Stock

Dozza. Monica Cavalletti / Adobe Stock

Badlands Park) in the province of Bologna. It's a park containing a karst or area of limestone, noted for its caves, remains of various villages and fascinating rock formations. See **www.emiliaromagnaturismo.it** and **www.visitmodena.it**

- Wander around the medieval town of Dozza, 6km south of Bologna. It's famous for its street art or murales, some of them by prestigious international names. **www.emiliaromagnaturismo.it**

GETTING HERE AND GETTING AROUND

Flights go to Bologna airport, and indeed Bologna is the perfect place to start. Trains run from Bologna to Pianoro, Badolo, Sasso Marconi and other local stations. Check **www.trenitalia.it** to plan your journey.

TUSCANY AND THE WAY TO ROME

→ Via Francigena – Canterbury to Rome
 • San Gimignano to Monteriggioni
→ Via Romea Germanica – Stade to Rome
 • Castiglion Fiorentino to Cortona
→ Via Romea Sanese – Florence to Siena

INTRODUCTION

Without doubt Tuscany is one of Italy's most loved regions in terms of its artistic and cultural treasures, its landscapes, traditions, and of course its food. It's a region which has seen the Etruscans, the Romans, the republics of the Middle Ages and the cultural explosion of the Renaissance. It has so much to offer the people who visit, its cities of art, its wines, and those views of vineyards, olive groves and cypresses that make up its countryside. Walk through Tuscany and you're giving yourself a chance to notice the details, those things that stay with us for years to come and make up our travel memories.

What is also so fascinating about Tuscany is its history. If we go back to the Middle Ages, we're in the age of the republics: the Republic of Pisa, and the Republics of Florence, Siena and Lucca. The Republic of Pisa was one of Italy's four most important maritime republics, along with Genoa, Venice and Amalfi. By the thirteenth century, the Republic of Florence had conquered most of Tuscany, while Siena and Lucca held firm. In 1406 it also took control of Pisa. During the Renaissance Florence was controlled by the powerful Medici family, thought to be originally from the valley of Mugello to the north of Florence. It was under this family that Florence became the birthplace of the Renaissance.

Knostiantyn / Adobe Stock

The Medici had made their wealth through banking and commerce in the Florence of the thirteenth century. In 1434 Cosimo de' Medici came to power as Lord of Florence. The House of Medici would rule Florence for nearly three hundred years. They expressed their power through art and architecture, and it was they who sponsored many of the Renaissance artists and architects whose works we now enjoy.

The effects of the Renaissance were felt in towns and cities all over Italy and Europe, and influenced the arts and sciences in all their forms. This is the age of Leonardo da Vinci, who came from Vinci to the west of Florence and lived at both the court of the Medicis and that of Ludovico the Moor, Duke of Milan. He left us works such as *The Last Supper* at the Basilica di Santa Maria delle Grazie in Milan, the *Mona Lisa,* now at the Louvre in Paris, and *The Annunciation*, *The Baptism of Christ* and *The Adoration of the Magi.* You can see the last three at the Uffizi Gallery in Florence. Speaking of which, do allow yourself time to visit Florence. Both the city and the Uffizi Gallery really are as wonderful as they say, and it will give you a good idea of painting and life more generally from this period. Make sure you visit the 'Primitivi' rooms at the Uffizi Gallery. They have medieval paintings dating from the thirteenth century by artists which include Giotto, Cimabue and Duccio di Buoninsegna. Medieval painting often had religious themes, just as the medieval literature of Geoffrey Chaucer tells of pilgrims in his *The Canterbury Tales*. Chaucer's tales may be more worldly and sometimes bawdy, but they still emphasise how how incredibly important religion was during the Middle Ages and this was reflected through the arts, and above all painting. Paintings were often elaborate and finely decorated using precious materials. When portraits were made of important society figures, this use of precious materials served to emphasise their status and wealth. When Giotto came along, things started to change. He introduced naturalism, the idea of spatial construction – basically, the fact that a painting is set within a specific space – and the expression of emotion. All this signified a move towards the Renaissance, and indeed Giotto is considered to be one of the first artists of the Renaissance. After the period of the Middle Ages, the Renaissance looked back to the classical period in terms of art and literature. It gave us some of the greatest artists, writers, scientists, astronomers and thinkers who shaped the world as we know it today. The Renaissance man found its ultimate expression in Leonardo da Vinci, the man who excelled in everything and left the world so many treasures. When you walk through the Tuscan countryside, you are walking through the history of all this.

Whether our pilgrim was walking the Via Francigena, the Via Romea Germanica or the Via Romea Sanese, which then linked with the Via Francigena, their goal was of course Rome, and a goal towards which they were slowly getting nearer. Of course, most of us will never reach Rome. You may well have a different goal, the chance to immerse yourself in so much beauty, history and religious history, and to discover it all slowly, step by step. This is the Tuscany we all know and love, and the region which has enchanted so many over the centuries.

LOCAL FOOD

The diet in the Middle Ages was plain, with cereals such as *farro* (spelt) and *orzo* (barley), vegetables, bread, which was also made of barley, and legumes.[1] *Salumi* and cheese[1] were also eaten. To get nearer to the medieval experience, try the Tuscan soups such as *ribollita*. It's made of stale bread and cabbage, boiled twice hence the name, and is delicious. Also try the chickpea (*ceci*) and lentil (*lenticchie*) soups. *Pappa di pomodoro* is historically a

Pici al ragù. Rachael Martin

poor man's dish. It's mainly found in the area around Florence, although remember that tomatoes didn't arrive in Italy until later, and in Tuscany until 1548 in Pisa. The story goes that Cosimo de Medici's wife Elenonora di Toldeo was given seeds by her father, Viceroy of the Kingdom of Naples. They were then grown and presented to her husband. *Pappa di pomodoro* is a Tuscan favourite, prepared with leftover bread, tomatoes, garlic and oil and cooked. *Panzanella* is the summer version with fresh tomatoes, onions and basil. The bread here is always made without salt, a leftover of twelfth century rivalry between Florence and Pisa. Pisa cut off the salt supply and so the Florentines started making bread without salt. Try the bread as *crostini di salsa di fegatini di pollo*, toasted bread dressed with a chicken liver paste, or a classic *bruschetta* with garlic, tomatoes and olive oil. The *salumi* here include *Prosciutto Toscano* which has a more pronounced flavour than that of Parma ham, the *sorprassata* salami, and *finocchiona*, which is a salami flavoured with fennel seeds and red wine. *Lardo di Colonnata* is the type of lard here, served sliced. As far as cheese goes, don't leave without trying the *Pecorino Toscano*. Pasta dishes include *tagliatelle al ragù di cinghiale*, tagliatelle in a wild boar ragù. *Pici* is a long thick pasta that's a bit like spaghetti but wider. Try *pici al ragù* or *pici all'aglione*, with a tomato, chilli and garlic sauce. The *aglione* comes from the type of garlic used. The famous meat dish here is the Fiorentina steak from local Chianina beef. Also try *peposo*, a local beef stew. For dessert, go for the sweet wine Vin Santo and *cantuccini* biscuits. When in Siena, try *panforte*, and *ricciarelli* biscuits.

VIA FRANCIGENA

We left our pilgrims up along the Via Francigena in the town of Echevennoz in the Aosta Valley, or maybe some of them walked further and arrived at the region's capital of Aosta. After, they went on to Pont Saint Martin with its Roman bridge, into Piedmont at the town of Ivrea. After, it was on to Vercelli, which is now famous for its rice fields where the rice is grown for the risottos that are eaten all over northern Italy. They then came into Lombardy, once known as Longobardia after the Longobards who lived there. They crossed the River Lambro in Lodi and walked on to Piacenza and Fidenza in Emilia-Romagna. Then they went up across the Appenine Mountains over the Passo della Cisa (Cisa Pass) to Pontremoli.

We join them again in Tuscany. We're in the area known as the Lunigiana,

San Miniato. hibiscus81 / Adobe Stock

once a Roman colony known as Luni and famous for its port. It's a lesser-known region in the Alpi Apuane, which are part of the northern Appenines. The Lunigiana is in both Tuscany in the north and Liguria in the south, and is famous for its medieval villages, churches and castles. The walk here goes along the valley Val di Magra, into Liguria around Sarzana and then back into Tuscany to Massa. Along with the nearby town of Carrara, Massa is famous for the marble quarries. The marble of Carrara has been used for centuries. The Romans used it for the Pantheon, while Michelangelo used it for his statue of David. After Massa, our pilgrims go south to Camaiore and come in to the beautiful city of Lucca, with its many churches.

Lucca was an important city during the Middle Ages because of its trade and the fact that the Via Francigena passed through it. Pilgrimages were acts of devotion, but they were also big business for the places the pilgrims travelled through. Pilgrims brought money for lodgings, food and guides, and as a result the city of Lucca was able to undertake a lot of urban replanning, the results of which we see today. The town has kept its medieval plan, with its four-kilometre-long Renaissance walls and city gates. Don't forget to see the Piazza dell'Anfiteatro, the main square which was built in the first half of the nineteenth century where the Roman amphitheatre used to

be. Visit the city's cathedral, the Duomo di San Martino. The original church dates back to the seventh century and the Irish bishop Saint Frediano, also known as St Frigidanus. It became a cathedral in the eighth century, while the cathedral dates from the eleventh century. The cathedral was an important stop for any pilgrim, and especially because it's home to the eighth century sculpture known as the *Volto Sacro* or the Holy Face, the oldest wooden sculpture in Europe.

From Lucca, our pilgrims made their way south to Altopascio. The forests here were notorious for bandits, which highlights the risks pilgrims took when they made their journeys. Going on a pilgrimage was quite simply a dangerous undertaking. You weren't guaranteed to get past any bandits alive, and even when you did there was always the risk of illness, bad weather which gave you other various illnesses and general aches and pains. If you were really unlucky, you might also be living through a plague. Nevertheless, arriving in San Miniato, a charming hilltop village famous for its truffles, must have been a welcome sight. It's in San Miniato that the Via Francigena crosses with one of the other important European pilgrimage routes; the Via Romea Strata. While the Via Francigena came down from Canterbury and through France and Switzerland, the Via Romea Strata brings together routes which came from the Baltic Sea through

Estonia, Latvia, Lithuania, Poland, the Czech Republic and Austria. It must have made for an incredible mix of cultures and languages along the streets of San Miniato.

Moving onwards, there's the church known as La Pieve di Santa Maria Assunta a Chianni. It's just outside the historical centre of Gambassi Terme and is one of the churches Sigeric mentions. It was the twentieth stop on his journey. There's also a third route which passes through here, the ancient Via Volterrana, the Etruscan road that linked Fiesole with Volterra. The Via Volterrana was a salt route. Volterra was famous for its salt which came from the natural lakes in the area, and the salt was taken via San Gimignano and on to Fiesole, and then to Florence and the surrounding area. Gambassi is famous for its spa waters with their healing properties, and a visit to the Termi di Gambassi is more than welcome after any walking. After this, the routes heads towards San Gimignano, with its magnificent skyline of towers. The Via Francigena in Tuscany is 220km long and is one of the most popular sections in Italy. You'll very probably meet plenty of other pilgrims or wayfarers as you walk, and it's this that really makes the walk: that sharing of experiences and exchanging advice, just as pilgrims would have done during the Middle Ages.

Termi di Gambassi, Piazza G. Di Vittorio, 1, Gambassi Termi www.termidigambassi.it

From San Gimignano to Monteriggioni

The route from San Gimignano to Monteriggioni is the 32nd stage of the Via Francigena. It's 31km long, takes about seven to eight hours, and is of medium difficulty because of its length and the 500m difference in altitude. It's also said by many to be the most beautiful stretch which passes through Tuscany, so if you're wanting to choose just one stretch of the walk, this is the one to do. San Gimignano itself is a medieval work of art. Its towers are a much-loved symbol of Tuscany, and it's no surprise that it's been a UNESCO World Heritage Site since 1990. The town had seventy-two tower houses in all. Fourteen remain today, some of which reach a height of 50 metres. All were built by noble families as a sign of their power and wealth. After you leave San Gimignano, follow the signs to Molino d'Aiano, which was mentioned by Sigeric in his diary.[2] The route continues past the Romanesque abbey, the Abbazzia di Santa Maria Assunta in Coneo, which was built around the year 1000 as an abbey for Benedictine monks. It's easy to imagine our pilgrims coming across this abbey and feeling it to be a welcome sight. Abbeys and monasteries always welcomed pilgrims and Benedictine monks were renowned for their hospitality. It was part of the Rule of St Benedict which they lived by. After food, rest and sleep, they were then ready to set off again. The next church along the way is the twelfth century Chiesa San Martino in Strove. It's also where you'll find the Locanda di Strove, which is a great place for you to have something to eat or stock up on provisions at their shop.

Then it's onwards to Monteriggioni. This fortified castle was built in the thirteenth century by the Republic of Siena as part of its defences against the Republic of Florence. There it is, up on its hill, still surrounded by its original walls, the same Monteriggioni

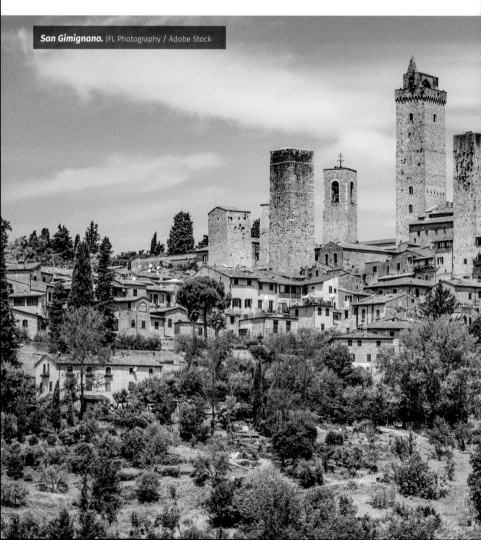

San Gimignano. JFL Photography / Adobe Stock

mentioned by Dante Alighieri in his *Divine Comedy*. (Inferno, Canto XXXI, verses 40-45 if you wish to go look it up.) If you'd like to do the whole walk you should allow seven to eight hours, although of course you can always just walk part of it and reward yourself with a typical Tuscan lunch!

After Monteriggioni, the walk continues to Siena and into the beautiful valley of Val d'Orcia with its rolling hills and soft landscapes. Then it's over into Lazio, and on to Rome.

Eat

Bear in mind that both San Gimignano and Monteriggioni are extremely popular in terms of food and accommodation, so expect to pay slightly more and for places to be booked up in advance. If you're hiring a car and thinking of walking parts of the walk in a day, then it's definitely worth considering other locations as a base.

San Gimignano
Osteria San Giovanni

Come for typical Tuscan dishes in the centre of San Gimignano. The restaurant has tables outside in the square, which make for a magical atmosphere in the evening.

Via San Giovanni, 6, San Gimignano
Facebook @Osteria San Giovanni

Spizziccheria Le Cicche Toscane

Una ciccha or *cicche* in the plural, is something beautiful or precious. In this case, it refers to the wonderful dishes served up at this charming restaurant in the centre. Try the boards of *salumi* (local cured meats), cheeses, salads and Tuscan specialities such as *pici al ragù bianco di Chianina*. The local pasta *pici* is served in a meat ragù sauce without tomatoes. That's why it's *bianco* or white. Also look out for their *pappa al pomodoro*.

Via San Martino, 5, San Gimignano
Facebook @ Spizzicheria Le Cicche Toscane

Monteriggioni
Trattoria Rigoletto

Just outside the walls, Trattoria Rigoletto offers Tuscan cooking with a view across the Tuscan countryside.

Viale Roma, 23, San Gimignano
Facebook @ Trattoria Rigoletto

Along the way
Il Castelletto, Colle di Val d'Elsa

Set in a medieval-style castle built in the 1920s, complete with turret, the atmosphere inside is a throwback to the twentieth century industrial history of Colle di Val d'Elsa. The menu includes traditional Tuscan favourites made with local produce. They also have a special menu for pilgrims and wayfarers.

Viale della Rimembranza, 1,
Colle di Val d'Elsa
www.ilcastellocolle.it

Locanda di Strove

The Locanda di Strove is always a welcome stop and offers Tuscan traditional favourites, pizza and homemade pasta dishes. They also have a shop for groceries.

Via XVII Marzo, Strove
www.locandadistrove.it

Stay

Wherever you are in Italy, it's always worth seeing if there's any accommodation run by religious orders as the accommodation is often

Val d'Elsa

The beautiful Val d'Elsa fulfils all the Tuscan stereotypes, with its rolling hills and River Elsa flowing through it. It was once home to the Etruscans, the ancient people who lived in Etruria. Etruria was an area which covered Tuscany, western Umbria and northern and central Lazio, pretty much the area between the River Arno and the River Tiber. They lived here for several hundred years until the Romans took power from the fourth century onwards. In fact the name Tuscany comes from the Etruscans or *Tusci* as the Romans called them at the time. They were well known for their craftsmanship and artisan skills, as well as their architecture and jewellery. Explore their history and visit the Archeological Park of Dometaia in Colle di Val d'Elsa. It has fifty-six Etruscan tombs from the 6th to 2nd centuries BC, some of which belonged to Etruscan nobles. If you want to look at the artefacts which were found there, visit the Archeological Museum Ranuccio Bianchi Bandinelli. The Archeological Museum in San Gimignano also has a selection of Etruscan finds, alongside Roman and medieval artefacts.

www.visitcolledivaldelsa.com/en/archaeological-park-of-dometaia
Archeological Museum Ranuccio Bianchi Bandinelli www.museisenesi.org/en/
Archeological Museum San Gimignano www.sangimignanomusei.it/eng/index.htm

Colle di Val d'Elsa. nejdetduzen / Adobe Stock

excellent, albeit sometimes simple. They may also offer honest, home cooking at a reasonable price. Do bear in mind that as a result, these places do fill up quick, so you will have to book in advance.

San Gimignano
Monastero San Gerolamo
Stay at this Benedictine monastery where accommodation is offered by the nuns who live there. For information, write to monasterosangimignano@gmail.com

Monache Benedettine Vallambrosane, Via Folgore 30

B&B Donna Nobile
Bed and breakfast with rooms in the historical centre of San Gimignano. They also have a cottage situated in the small hamlet of San Donato if you're looking for a base from which to go off and walk.

Via delle Romite, 15/21/25
www.donnanobile.it

Monteriggioni
Casa per ferie Santa Maria Assunta
This religious property offers accommodation, spiritual retreats and spiritual exercise inside the walls. Rooms are double, triple and multiple.

Their website is also a great source of addresses for other religious accommodation in the area.

Piazza Dante Aligleiri, 23
www.ospitalitareligiosa.it

Rooms and Wine
Sleep in the heart of Monteriggioni in a seventh century palazzo which also happens to be the tallest in the village and offers wonderful views of both fortress and countryside.

Via Ava dei Lambardi, 1
www.roomsandwine.com

Maps, Links and Useful Information
Tuscany
www.visittuscany.com is the official website for Tuscany. Also see www.italia.it/en/tuscany and www.discovertuscany.com

Via Francigena
www.viefrancigene.org is the official website which includes routes, maps,

guides, apps and practical information. Also download the app Via Francigena - Official App.

Lucca
See www.turismo.lucca.it for information about what to do and see in Lucca.

San Gimignano
See www.sangimignano.com for information about what to do and see in San Gimignano.

When to go
Avoid the crowds and the summer heat and come in spring or autumn.

While You're Here

- Visit the Oasi del Bottaccio and its lake Lago della Gherardesca. The oasis is a WWF protected area and home to migrant birds such as cormorants, herons and ducks. Lake Gherardesca is what is left of what was once a much larger lake, what the Pisans and Florentines called Lake Bientina and what the people of Lucca called Lake Sesto. It's beautiful walking country with huts for birdwatching. www.cappanori-terraditoscana.org
- The Castelvecchio Nature Reserve is in the Alta Valdelsa near San Gimignano and is home to various animals and birds

Lago della Gherardesca.
Marco Taliani / Adobe Stock

Sentierelsa in the Valdelsa River Park. filippoph / Adobe Stock

such as foxes, wild boars, deers, hares, hawks, pheasants and partridges. Walk through the beautiful woods and visit the medieval ruins of the Castrum Vetus or Castelvecchio, the old castle. For an interactive map, see www.parks.it/riserva.castelvecchio.

- Sentierelsa is the walk along the River Elsa, which is known for its turquoise waters. The walk is 4km long and suitable for all. Along here you'll see a hydraulic system which was renovated by the Grand Duke of Tuscany Ferdinand I de' Medici. In summer you can also bathe in the river. What better way to spend a summer's afternoon than with a walk and a picnic by a river in Tuscany? www.visitcolledivaldelsa.com/en/elsa-river-trail-sentierelsa

VIA ROMEA GERMANICA

We left the Via Romea Germanica near Ferrara in the Valli di Comacchio on the coast in Emilia Romagna. After walking through the flatlands of this area and visiting the mosaics of Ravenna, our pilgrims then headed inland towards Forlimpopoli and the Roman town of Forlì. They might have stopped off at the Romanesque Basilica di San Mercuriale with its twelfth century bell tower. The path then starts to go up into the hills to Cusercoli. What were our pilgrims thinking when they looked up at the Appenine Mountains in front of them? Some of them may have come all the way from Stade, others from places along the way in Germany. Some may have started their journey in what we now call Italy. They had very probably all faced various hardships in some form. Yet they were still here, still on their journeys. It's an incredible feat when you think about it. Some of us have already experienced getting halfway up a mountain, looking upwards at how far we still need to go, and feeling our heart sink. I know I have, and then I've pulled myself together as they say, gathered all my courage, and kept going. That's what it's all about, the just keeping going. I like to think of our medieval pilgrims as doing the same. When they felt like all the odds were against them, they just kept going.

stevanzz / Adobe Stock

There our pilgrims were, in or near Bagno Romana going across the Tuscan-Emilian Appenines at the Passo Serra mountain pass that goes into the valley of Vallesanta (Saint's Valley) in Tuscany. This last stretch from Bagno di Romagna is hard. It involves a difference in altitude of over 1,200m but it's also an extremely beautiful area with its forests and remote villages. This is also the Flaminia Minor route that Roman armies used. Like many remote sections of the routes which the pilgrims followed, there was safety in numbers, and pilgrims often gathered in groups to protect themselves from all the bandits. Chitignano slightly further on was known for the smuggling of gunpowder and cigars. At this time there was a castle in the valley at Montefatucchio but all traces of it have now disappeared. At Alpe di Serra, the road goes off to La Verna, the Franciscan sanctuary associated with Saint Francis, where he received his stigmata in September 1224. It's a very special place, immersed in nature. It does get busy though as it's one of the most popular destinations for pilgrims from all over the world. The Vallesanta takes its name from Saint Francis. You can read more about Saint Francis and La Verna in the next chapter.

When you get to Vallesanta, you're now in the Casentino, one of the four valleys of the province of Arezzo. The Casentinesi Forests National Park is the park here which was founded in 1993 along the Tuscan-Romagnolo Appenines to protect the beech forests. They now have UNESCO world heritage status. It's one of the largest areas of forests in Europe and straddles both Emilia-Romagna and Tuscany. It's home to fallow roe deer, wolves and wild boar, while on the Romagna side you might also see golden eagles, peregrine falcons and eagle owls.[3] From here the route continues through the province of Arezzo as far as Cortona, and then it's on to Pozzuolo, a hamlet of Castiglione del Lago near Lake Trasimeno. For the modern tourist, Lake Trasimeno is a sight to soothe sore, tired eyes, and the perfect place to spend a day relaxing. At this point you're now in Umbria and 268km from Rome.

The whole stretch of the Via Romea Germanica in Tuscany from Bagno di Romagna to Pozzuolo is 142km and split into seven stages, so if you're planning to do it all, then calculate roughly a day for each stage. Alternatively, pick sections as you please. It's a wonderful way to explore Tuscany's sometimes lesser-known valleys and really soak up those views and atmosphere.

From Castiglion Fiorentino to Cortona
If you choose one stage of the walk, then choose this for views of the Val di Chiana and the town of Cortona up on the hill at the end of it. Yes, you will be walking uphill just as you feel you're

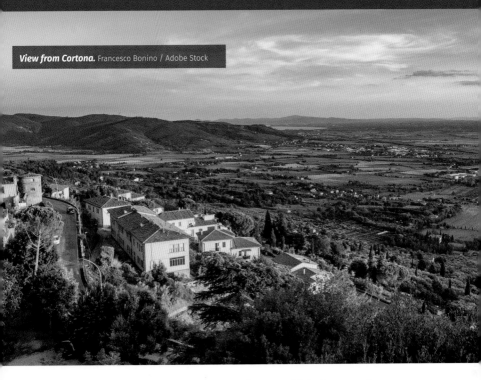

View from Cortona. Francesco Bonino / Adobe Stock

nearing the end, but trust me when I say it will be worth it. Also book a table at Osteria del Teatro for the evening you get there to really complete the experience. Cortona shot to fame when Frances Mayes wrote about doing up a property here. A film was later made, and the result was that the town become very popular with tourists. It's still beautiful though, and merits a place on any tourist's travel itinerary, especially if you've never visited this area of Tuscany before. Combine it with a few days in Arezzo if you can.

The whole walk is 13km long and marked as easy. Castiglion Fiorentino and Cortona are both medieval hilltop villages which deserve time, so you could spend a day in Castiglion Fiorentino and then set off and walk to Cortona the next day. Then give yourself the day after to enjoy Cortona. The point is not to rush, to give yourself the time to take it all in slowly. The walk takes you through the Valdichiana, once part of the region where the Etruscans lived. When the Romans arrived, they made good use of the River Clanis which used to flow through the valley and built various river ports so that they could transport goods. It's now closely associated with an ancient breed of cow known as the Chiana, which is prized for its meat. The famous Florentine steak known as the *Fiorentina* is always Chiana meat.

Eat

Wherever you go, make sure you try the local *pici*, a thick hand-rolled spaghetti made of flour, water and salt and very typical of the area. They're served *all'Aglione*, in a tomato sauce with aglione, a type of garlic, in a duck or 'nana' sauce, and with a meat ragù, usually Chiana meat cooked with Chianti wine. It's the perfect lunch or dinner after all the walking!

Castiglion Fiorentino
Ristorante Da Muzzicone
This typical Tuscan restaurant with terrace serves local pasta and meat dishes such as the famous Fiorentina steak, tagliata and fillet steak.

Via San Francesco, 7

Cortona
Osteria del Teatro
This characteristic osteria in a restored sixteenth century building in the centre of Cortona has been serving local Tuscan dishes since 1994. They also have their own products including olive oil and wine for you to take home with you. It's definitely one to put on your list!

Via Giuseppe Maffei, 2
www.osteria-de-teatro.com

Arezzo

The main town in the Val di Chiana or Valdichiana is Arezzo. It was one of the twelve Etruscan city states, and later a Roman town called Arretium. In the Middle Ages, it was one of the most important towns occupied by the Longobards who built castles and churches there, while the Renaissance saw a series of frescoes commissioned in the Basilica di San Francesco. The frescoes became known as *The Legend of the True Cross*. They were painted by Piero della Francesca and are considered masterpieces of the Renaissance period. Arezzo's main square is the Piazza Grande or Piazza Vassari, which featured in Roberto Benigni's film *La Vita è Bella* and is said to be one of Italy's most beautiful. The town's most famous sons are poet, writer and philosopher Petrarch, and painter and architect Giorgio Vasari. Petrarch was born here on 20 July 1304 and you can visit his house, the Accademia Petrarca, now a museum which celebrates his life. Vasari was born here two hundred years later in 1511. You can also visit his house, the Casa-Museo di Giorgio Vasari, and above all see his contributions to the town. His artistic works include the *Deposition from the Cross* in the Chiesa della Santissima Annunziata and the *Crowning of the Virgin* in the Chiesa di Santa Flora e Lucilla. Also visit the Museum of Medieval and Modern Art for his *Madonna with Child* and *Saint John the Baptist*. Vasari was also the architect behind the Palazzo delle Logge in Piazza Grande and the bell tower of the Palazzo della Fraternità dei Laici. If you're there on the first weekend of the month, the town holds its antiques fair, which all just adds to the character of this beautiful town. Arezzo is sometimes overlooked for other Tuscan destinations, which just makes it more appealing for those of us who want to slow it all down, enjoy that cappuccino in the square and watch this Tuscan world go by. You can get a real feeling about a place from sitting in cafés in squares!

Arezzo. daskeleineatelier / Adobe Stock

Taverna Pane e Vino

This restaurant and winery in Piazza Signorelli serves local dishes, *bruschetta* and boards of *salumi* (cured meats).

Piazza Signorelli, 27
www.pane-vino.it

Stay

Castiglion Fiorentino
B&B La Casa del Frate

Just a five minute walk from the station and its links with Florence and Rome, this charming bed and breakfast has welcoming rooms with views of the garden.

Via Camillo Benso Conte di Cavour, 59

Cortona
B&B Locanda Pane e Vino

This bed and breakfast is situated in a watch tower and belongs to the same people who have the Taverna Pane e Vino. They also have apartments.

Vicolo San Giovanni, 10
www.pane-vino.it

Villa Santa Margherita

Villa Santa Margherita is a guest house run by the nuns of the Serve di Maria Reparatrice order. They offer bed and breakfast accommodation just outside the walls of the town.

Viale Cesare Battisti, 17
www.villasantamargheritacortona.it

Please note that the website is in Italian. For bookings, write to info@villasantamargheritacortona.it

Maps, Links and Useful Information

Tuscany

www.visittuscany.com is the official website for Tuscany. Also see www.italia.it/en/tuscany and www.discovertuscany.com

Via Romea Germanica

www.viaromeagermanica.com is the official website with routes, maps, guides, apps and practical information. Also download the app Via Francigena - Official App.

Valdichiana

See www.valdichianinaliving.it for information about what to do and see. They also have information about various tours and experiences.

Cortona

See www.cortonamia.com for information about what to do and see. There's always plenty going on in Cortona, so make sure to check out the events section.

Arezzo

www.visitarezzo.com has information about the town, and its various historical re-enactments and events.

When to go

Bear in mind that all of Tuscany can get extremely busy and hot in summer, so spring and autumn are better times to visit, especially if you're planning to do a lot of walking.

While You're Here

- The Sentiero della Bonifica is the 62km long cycle footpath which goes along the Maestro della Chiana canal and joins Arezzo with Chiusi. It's a flat walk that is suitable for all, and the perfect way to spend a day out enjoying the Valdichiana countryside. For maps and itineraries see **www.sentierodellabonifica.it**
- The Sentiero del Vinsanto follows the medieval route which linked the castle of Torrita di Siena, scene of the famous fourteenth century Battle of Torrita, with the castle of Montefollonico. The path takes its name from the Vin Santo dessert wine which is produced in the area and traditionally eaten with cantuccini biscuits. The walk is 7km long and rated easy. Take a picnic and eat at one of the five picnic areas, and don't forget your Vin Santo and *cantuccini* biscuits! The walk begins at the camper area in Torrita di Siena and ends in the beautiful *borgo* or characteristic village of Montefollonico at the medieval gate, the Porta di Follonico.
- Spend a few days exploring the Casentinesi Forests National Park. Its official title is Parco Nazionale delle Foreste Casentinesi, Monte Falterona e Campigna.

Montepulciano. LianeM / Adobe Stock

Camaldoli. adistock / Adobe Stock

- The mountain known as Monte Falterona is where the River Arno begins, the river most famously associated with Florence. In ancient times it was said to be sacred, and according to the Etruscans, the lake up there known as Lago degli Idoli (Lake of the Idols) had healing powers. It's an important Etruscan archeological site and surrounded by wonderful walking country. Campigna on the other hand is the highest and smallest village in the Valle del Bidente, over in Emilia-Romagna. Visit the Sanctuary of La Verna where Saint Francis received his stigmata and the Camaldoli Monastery which was founded in 1012 by Saint Romualdo. Romualdo was a Benedictine monk who founded the Camoldolese Order, which involved an austere and hermetical life. It's easy to see why the Casentino was chosen as a place for religious life and reflection. The natural beauty all around makes it the perfect setting. See www.ilbelcasentino.it for details of walks, and the next chapter for the life of Saint Francis.

- Head to Montepulciano in the part of the Valdichiana in the province of Siena. This stunning medieval hilltop village with its beautiful Piazza Grande is famous for the Vino Nobile del Montepulciano, and in fact this is where the path known as the Sentiero del Nobile gets its name. It starts at the Chiesa di Sant'Agnese in Montepulciano and passes by the vineyards, olive groves and Lake Montepulciano. It's 18km long with a difference in altitude of 600km. For further information and itinerary, see www.stradedisiena.it/en/thenobile-trail For wine tasting, www.stradadelnobile.it is the association of local wine producers, farms and restaurants, and has a list of both vineyards and wine shops. They also have details of wine tours and cooking classes.

- If you don't fancy doing the whole Sentiero del Nobile, spend a day at the nature reserve of Lake Montepulciano with its impressive range of flora and fauna. For further information, see www.riservalagodimontepulciano.it

VIA ROMEA SANESE

The Via Romea Sanese links Florence with Siena and just as its name implies, ultimately Rome. It was originally called Via Sanctus Donatus in Pocis in reference to San Donato di Poggio through which it goes, hence Via Sanese. It passes through the Chianti region from which it also takes its name. It starts in Florence at the Piazza della Santissima Annunziata and takes you across Florence past some of the city's most important sights before you leave. It finishes at the Basilica di San Francesco in Siena. Since 1996 the historical centre of Siena has been a UNESCO World Heritage site. It really is a medieval jewel in the middle of the Tuscan countryside. It's also here in Siena that it meets the Via Francigena along Viale Cavour. From here, it's up to you. Either pick up the Via Francigena and keep going onwards to Rome or spend time in Siena and the surrounding area. Whichever you decide, it's certainly worth taking time to see Siena. It's rich in history and artistic and architectural delights, and home to historical re-enactments such as the medieval horse race, the Palio. Think of Siena as the icing on the cake when you reach the end of your walk, up there on its hill surrounded by its city walls and with so much beauty within it. In the meantime, there is also so much more to see.

The walk is 78km long, for the most part footpaths and tracks, and is in four stages. For our medieval pilgrim, the emphasis was on the churches. For today's walker, it's also possible that it's the wine that's a big attraction, although it's very probable that our medieval pilgrim enjoyed a glass or a few. Documents dating back to the thirteenth century already mention the production of a wine called Chianti, although the roots of wine production here probably go as far back as the Etruscans. Whether you're here as pilgrim or walker, this is the ideal route for mixing the spiritual with the

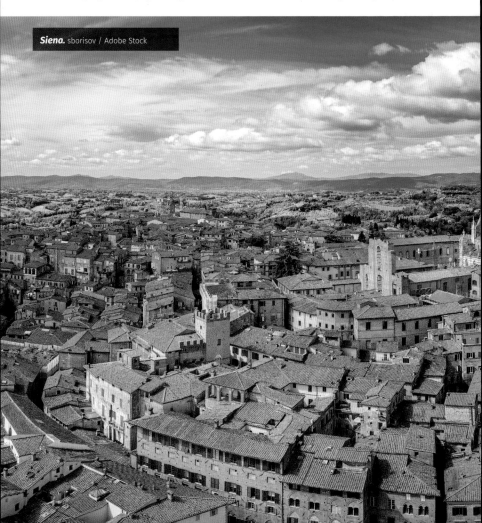

Siena. sborisov / Adobe Stock

worldly, and soaking up those views as you go. The walk passes through three of the municipalities where the Chianti Classico wine is produced. Note that this is Chianti Classico and not Chianti. There is a difference. Chianti Classico is produced in the historical area where Chianti was produced, whereas Chianti

can be produced outside this region. Basically, the walk takes you through the Chianti heartland. I mean really, what more could you wish for?

As you leave Florence through the Porta San Miniato and go south, you'll pass by the Chiesa di San Felice a Ema, and the Albergaccio in Sant'Andrea in Percussina, a hamlet of San Casciano in Val di Pesa. The Albergaccio was home to Niccolò Macchiavelli when he was sent into exile by the Medici family. Machiavelli was accused of plotting against the De Medicis, found innocent but still sent away from Florence. It was here that he wrote two of his most important works, his *Discourses on Livy* and *The Prince*. The next village is San Casciano in Val di Pesa, once an important *mansio* (road station) in Roman times, and essential point for the protection of Florence. It marks the end of the first stage of the walk and the beginning of the Chianti Classico region. From here the route makes it way through the classic landscapes of the Chianti countryside with its vineyards and cypresses to Badia a Passignano, known for its eleventh century monastery. You'd be forgiven for mistaking it to be a castle with its fortified walls, but this was the home of monks of the Vallambrosian order. Like in many rural areas, the monks were responsible for improving local agriculture, which included terracing the vineyards and putting in irrigation systems. The medieval village of

San Donato in Poggio marks the next stage. It has a lovely Romanesque church which is still very much as it was when it was built. San Donato in Pioggio was an important stop for medieval pilgrims because of the hospital there. After this, it's on past vineyards and through woods to Castellina in Chianti and the beginning of the final stretch to Siena.

From Castellina in Chianti to Siena

Castellina in Chianti was an Etruscan town and is one of the main towns in the Chianti region. Its position between Florence and Siena meant that it was a desirable asset for both republics. The town's medieval castle is known as the Rocca, while the Via delle Volte was a covered walkway designed by Filippo Brunelleschi and used by the guards to defend the town from the people of Siena. It's now home to artisanal shops and restaurants. While you're here, look inside the archeological museum, the Museo Archeologico del Chianti and learn more about the region's history and its Etruscan past. Nearby Tumolo

Castellina in Chianti. Guido / Adobe Stock

di Montecalvario is a sixth century BC Etruscan tomb, while the Necropolis di Poggino in the hamlet of Fonterutoli is an Etruscan graveyard. You could easily spend a few days enjoying both town and the area before you set off on your walk.

The walk from Castellina in Chianti to Siena is 25km long and roughly takes six and a half hours. It's one of the tougher walks because of the considerable differences in altitude, but you can always just walk a section if you prefer. It takes you through Castellina in Chianti and Fonterutoli, site of an Etruscan necropolis, and the hamlets of Cappana, Casa Frassi and Casalino. The next hamlet, Quercegrossa, is part of the town of Monteriggioni, and was an important point of defence for the people of Siena against the Florentines. It's also where the Italian Renaissance sculptor Jacopo della Quercia was born in 1374. He went on to decorate the fountain in Piazza del Campo in Siena, which you can visit when you get to Siena. The Mulino di Quercegrossa here is a local agriturismo. If you want to take the walk more slowly, you might want to consider splitting the walk, in which case spend a night here and have a meal. From Quercegrossa it's on to Uopini and its church Chiesa di Santi Erasmo e Marcellino and then into Siena through the Antiporta di Camollia. It's the city's most external gate, hence antiporta, and was built in 1270. The walk then takes you through the centre of Siena where it finishes at the Basilica di San Francesco in Piazza San Francesco. It's an impressive sight as you walk towards one of Tuscany's most beautiful cities until you finally arrive and can enjoy and savour it all. Find a table in the sun and enjoy something cool.

Eat

Castellini in Chianti
Ristorante Sotto le Volte
Set under the covered walkway known as Via delle Volte, the restaurant offers traditional dishes such as *pappardelle con ragù di cinghiale* (wild boar ragù) and *pici con briciole di pane e mandorle tostate*, the local thick type of spaghetti with breadcrumbs and toasted almonds. Meat dishes include the local *peposo alla fornacina*, a beef stew cooked with plenty of pepper.

Via delle Volte, 14-16
www.sottolevolteristorante.it

Quercegrossa
Mulino di Quercegrossa
Eat at the agriturismo Mulino di Quercegrossa set in an old mill in the middle of the countryside. It's just a fifteen-minute walk from Quercegrossa. The menu has both local specialities and pizza cooked in traditional ovens. The atmosphere is very special,

particularly in the evening. They also have rooms (see below).

Località Mulino di Quercegrossa
www.mulinodiquercegrossa.it

Siena
Osteria del Castelvecchio
Senius and Ascanius, twin sons of Remus, fled after their uncle Romulus killed their father. They are said to be the founders of Siena, and the city's symbol is a she-wolf feeding them both. This is supposed to be the area of Siena where they came to. Try traditional dishes such as *pici al cinghiale*, pici with wild boar sauce, the famous Fiorentina steak and more. The restaurant also has an internal garden with tables outside.

Via Castelvecchio, 65

Stay
Castellini in Chianti
Mariani Bed and Breakfast
Just fifty metres away from the historical centre, this charming bed and breakfast with garden and terrace offers rooms with a view of the countryside and buffet breakfast.

Via della Remembranza, 70
www.bbmariani.it

Villa Cristina
Liberty style Villa Cristina offers bed and breakfast and is a five minute walk from the centre. They have six double

rooms all with private bathrooms and a garden with swimming pool.

Via Fiorentina, 34
www.villacristinachianti.it

Quercegrossa
Mulino di Quercegrossa
This is the same agriturismo as the restaurant. Rooms are decorated in the traditional style. There is also a seven-pool outdoor swimming complex known as Aqualis which is open during the summer months.

Località Mulino di Quercegrossa
www.mulinodiquercegrossa.it

Siena
Casa di Antonella
Casa di Antonella has five simple rooms with two shared bathrooms near the Piazza del Campo.

Via delle Terme, 72
www.beb.it/lacasadiantonellasiena

Antica Residenza Cicogna
This was the Cicogna family's winter residence for two centuries until the Second World War when the building was taken over and used to house the poor. Elisa is one of the family's descendants and has created a welcoming bed and breakfast with elegantly furnished rooms near the Piazza del Campo.

Via delle Terme, 76
www.anticaresidenzacicogna.it

Chianti

The area known as the Chianti is one of the most beautiful in Tuscany. It ticks all the boxes: vineyards, olive groves, hilltop medieval villages, churches, farmhouses, exquisite food, and wine which is famous throughout the world. It's literally a 20km long chain of hills or small mountains which passes through the provinces of Siena, Florence and Arezzo. The Lega del Chianti was founded in 1384 by the Republic of Florence. It was made up of Radda in Chianti, Gaiole in Chianti and Castellini in Chianti, and its symbol was a black cockerel which you'll find on bottles of Chianti Classico. While you're here, also visit Greve in Chianti, another medieval town which was fiercely contested by Siena and Florence. Relax at a bar under its covered walkway and visit the wine museum, the Museo del Vino, where you can explore wine making techniques of the past. They also offer wine tasting and a visit to the *Prosciuttaia* where the hams are kept. The nearby hamlet of Montefioralle is one of Italy's most beautiful *borghi* or villages, a fortified village which has kept its medieval atmosphere. The Vespucci family lived in the 10th century castle here, and of course Amerigo Vespucci was the navigator who discovered America. Today the castle often hosts wine tasting and gastronomical events.

www.museovino.it

stevanzz / Adobe Stock

Crete Senesi

Take time to visit the area known as the Crete Senesi, the clay hills south of Siena, which stretch across the provinces of Siena and Arezzo. *Creta* is a type of clay, and it's from this that they take their name. In the Middle Ages the area was known as the desert of Accona, which really gives an idea of how arid this area can appear. The landscape was formed between two and a half and four a half million years ago, an almost other-worldly landscape with cypresses and the odd village and farm. It's famous for its changes in colour according to season and time of day, and certainly worth spending a few days exploring. Buses go from Florence and Siena to the main towns of Buonconvento and Asciano, but it's a lot easier to get around if you hire a car. Make sure you visit the towns of Asciano and Buonconvento, but also take time to explore smaller towns such as San Giovanni d'Asso, Trequanda and Rapalano Terme. Also take a trip to the Abbey of Monte Oliveto Maggiore, which was founded in 1320 and still home to the Olivetan Benedictine monks today. The large cloister inside the monastery is famous for its *Stories of Saint Benedict* cycle of frescoes by Luca Signorelli. Finally, go for a walk! The local tourist site www.visitcretesenesi.it has itineraries and maps for exploring the region on foot. Also don't miss the Viale dei Cipressi, the iconic cypress-lined track often associated with Tuscany that goes off the Strada Provinciale 60 to the Podere Baccoleno farm.

Viale dei Cipressi. andanomala / Adobe Stock

Maps, Links and Useful Information

Tuscany
www.visittuscany.com is the official website for Tuscany. Also see www.italia.it/en/tuscany and www.discovertuscany.com

Via Romea Sanese (Via Romea del Chianti)
See www.visittuscany.com for maps and itineraries.

Florence
www.visitflorence.com and www.feelflorence.it are both good starting points for exploring the city.

Siena
www.visitsienaofficial.it is the official website.

Chianti
See www.visitchianit.net, www.chianti.com and www.chianti.info

for information about what to do and see. They also have information about various tours and experiences.

When to go
Spring and autumn are better times to visit as it's not as hot, and especially if you're planning to do a lot of walking.

GETTING HERE AND GETTING AROUND

Flights go to Florence and Pisa, and Rome has excellent rail links with Florence if you're thinking of flying in to Rome. Arezzo is also along the Milan – Rome train route which stops in Florence. There are also slower trains which stop at every station and are useful for getting to towns and villages between the main cities. Check www.trenitalia.it to plan your journey. Once you get there, also look into times and routes of local buses.

UMBRIA AND THE WAYS OF THE SAINTS

→ Via di San Francesco / Way of St Francis – Assisi to La Verna and Assisi to Rome
→ Cammino di San Benedetto / Way of St Benedict – Assisi to Montecassino

INTRODUCTION

The beautiful region of Umbria with its mountains and hills is in the centre of Italy and halfway between the Tyrrhenean Sea on the west and the Adriatic to the east. It's the heartland of two walks which celebrate the lives of two of Italy's most famous saints, Saint Francis of Assisi, and Saint Benedict of Norcia, the founder of western monasticism. It's one of the few Italian regions which doesn't border the sea and is often known as the *cuore verde* or green heart of Italy. The history of its people goes back to ancient times. Umbria takes its name from the ancient Umbri people. It is thought that they lived in the area east of the River Tiber from the First Iron Age. Later, the Etruscans arrived, and their main towns were Perugia or Perusna as they called

it, and Orvieto or Velzna. Both towns have Etruscan remains. Near Perugia there's the Palazzone Necropolis, an Etruscan cemetery, and the Volumni Hypogeum, the chamber which is the tomb of the Velimna family. In the city of Perguia itself you can see both the Etruscan Arch known as Porta Pulchra (the beautiful gate), and the Etruscan walls which date from the third and fourth centuries BC. There's also the third century BC Etruscan Well, a feat of Etruscan hydraulic engineering with its relative museum. Orvieto stands high up on its cliff known as the Rupe. It was the last Etruscan city to fall to the Romans when they took control of the territory towards the end of the third century BC. The Crocifisso del Tufo (Crucifix of the Tufo) is the Etruscan necropolis just outside the town at the bottom of the cliff. Visit the

The flowering plains of Castelluccio di Norcia. rudiernst / Adobe Stock

archaeological area of the Temple of Belvedere. The Claudia Faina Museum and Civic Archeological Museum also have Etruscan artefacts. The Romans travelled into Umbria via the Via Flaminia that linked Rome with Rimini. You can also explore the history of the Romans in towns such as Assisi, Gubbio and Spello. The Middle Ages saw the construction of fortified towns up on the hill, and Umbria has so many examples. The Renaissance was centred in Perugia, and Pietro di Cristoforo Vannucci, known as Perugino, is one of Perugia's most sons. He is most famous for his *Delivery of the Keys* on the wall of the Sistine Chapel in Rome.

Alongside this wealth of history, art and culture, Umbria offers landscapes of great natural beauty. There's the mountain plateau of Castelluccio di Norcia in the Monti Sibillini National Park, famous for the lentil and other flowers which blossom there between May and July, lakes such as Lake Trasimeno and Lake Piediluco, and the spectacular Marmore Falls, the largest man-made waterfalls in Europe that were made by the Romans near Terni. The Monti Sibillini National Park also stretches across into Le Marche and is named after an ancient sybil who lived up on the mountain and gave it its name. Umbria also has five regional parks and six mountains over 2,000 metres, the highest being Monte Vettore at 2,476m. It's home to the Tiber River Park, the same Tiber that goes to Rome. The park was given WWF protection in 1990 because of its biodiversity and wildlife. The Tiber is what initially attracted the Umbri and the Etruscans to settle in Umbria and build their communities along the river. Later, the Romans did the same.

All this is the stage for the lives of Saint Francis of Assisi and Saint Benedict of Norcia. The Way of Saint Francis and Way of Saint Benedict are both new walks which bring together significant places in the saints' lives. The Way of Saint Benedict is the work of Simone Frignani, who has both created new walks and mapped out the routes of old walks. His guide *The Way of Saint Benedict* is available in English and is the one to get if you're wanting to do the whole walk. For the Way of Saint Francis, see the guide *On the Road with Saint Francis* by Angela Maria Serracchioli. Both books are published by Terra di Mezzo Editore.

SAINT BENEDICT OF NORCIA

Saint Benedict was born in 480 into a Christian family of nobles. His father was a Roman Consul and General of the Roman army, and according to the tradition of the time he was sent to Rome with his twin sister Scolastica for his education. When he arrived

in Rome, he didn't particularly like what he saw. His fellow students were far from model students, often dedicated to living luxurious and self-indulgent lives, which was far from how Benedict imagined his own life. Still a teenager, he left his studies and decided to pursue a religious life in the mountains near Subiaco in the heart of the Regional Park of Monte Subiaco, about 70km from Rome. He spent three years living alone in a cave on Mount

Taleo, hidden away from the world. He dedicated his life to prayer and meditation in preparation for his life as a monk. This cave is now known as the Sanctuary of Sacro Speco, or the Holy Cave. When Benedict wrote his *Rule* in 530, he recognised the importance of organising monks into communities, in which they lived under the authority of an abbot. It established the rules of poverty, chastity and obedience. His motto was *ora et labora*, work and pray. He set up twelve monasteries in Subiaco, and then in 529 he left for Montecassino and set up his monastery there. He died in the Abbey of Montecassino in 547, forty days after his sister Scolastica, and they were both buried in the same tomb. He was canonized in 1220, and in 1964 he was declared patron saint of Europe by Pope Paolo VI in recognition of his influence on western culture and monasticism.

Subiaco. oltrelautostrada / Adobe Stock

SAINT FRANCIS OF ASSISI

Saint Francis was born in Assisi in 1181 or 1182 to a wealthy merchant family. He was all set to follow in his father's footsteps and enter the family business when he decided upon a military career. As a result, he spent a year as a prisoner of the Perugians in the war between Assisi and Perugia. He was twenty at the time and it was after this that he began to feel a religious calling. Instead of becoming a knight, he chose to follow a religious life. His aim was to live as closely as he could to the life of Christ by following the vows of poverty, chastity and obedience. He originally preached to people in the street, and then in 1209 he asked the Pope for permission to found his Franciscan Order. This order was originally made up of Saint Francis' followers in the local area. It then spread through the region and the rest of Italy. An order for nuns followed in 1212 when Saint Clare became the abbess of the first monastery of the Poor Ladies, who would later be known as the Poor Clares. Saint Francis was also a poet, and his famous *Canticle of the Creatures* illustrates the feelings he felt with nature and the connection of all nature with God. One of the most famous images is of him preaching to the birds. He was known for walking around in the brown robe and sandals he wore, the clothing which Franciscan monks still wear today. In 1213 Saint Francis

View of Assisi from Spello. crisfotolux / Adobe Stock

was given the chance to go up to Monte Penna to build a hermitage there. It was given to him by a Tuscan count, Orlando Cattani di Chiusi della Verna, who lived in the the village of Chiusi della Verna nearby. He used to go up there with his monks to pray and fast, and it was while he was here in summer 1224 that he asked God to let him share in the Passion of Christ. On 17 September 1224 he received the stigmata, wounds in his hands and feet and a gash in his side, the five wounds of Christ, which he would have until his death. He died on Saturday, 3 October 1226 at the age of forty-four and was canonised by Pope Gregory IX on 16 July 1228.

LOCAL FOOD

One of the typical antipasto here is *crostini*, served with black truffle, the speciality of Norcia, olive paste or a paste of chicken livers. *Bruschetta* are served with fresh tomatoes or with a drizzle of olive oil and pinch of salt. Try them to believe how good they can be. In Norcia, you'll find *stranghozzi*, also called *umbricelli* on the menus with a grating of black truffle. They're a bit like the Tuscan *pici* and also served with a rich tomato sauce or ragù. Also look out for *pappardelle al cinghiale*, pappardelle in a wild boar sauce. *Pasta alla norcina* is penne in a sauce of local

Pappardelle with wild boar sauce.
Comugnero Silvana / Adobe Stock

sausage and sheep's ricotta, sometimes with a grating of black truffle. The famous green lentils from Castelluccio di Norcia are used in the soup *zuppa di lenticchie di Castelluccio*. As far as cured meats are concerned, look out for *Prosciutto di Norcia, capocollo* which is what they call *coppa* around here, *salame al tartufo nero* di Norcia – salami with black truffle from Norcia, and *sanguinaccio*, made from offal and pig's blood. Cheeses to try include *pecorino di Norcia, ricotta salata di Norcia* and *caciotta di tartufo. Torta al testo* is also known as *crescia* or *ciaccia* and made to a very old recipe. It's a large round flat bread which, according to the traditional Umbrian recipe, has a filling of spinach and sausage but you'll also find it filled with ham or salami. Also try *panino alla porchetta*, de-boned roast pork cooked with herbs and sliced thick into sandwiches. Both are tasty and filling snacks if you're looking for something quick and easy as you walk. Cakes and desserts include *rocciata* from Assisi. It looks a bit like a strudel but is filled with nuts and raisins. *Baci di Assisi* are soft biscuits covered with almonds, while *pampetato* is the traditional round cake made with pine nuts, almonds, nuts and raisins. There's a lot to try and it doesn't have to prove expensive. Some of the best eating experiences I've had consisted of bread filled with the local *salumi* while out walking. It can give a whole new meaning to the idea of lunch with a view!

LA VIA DI FRANCESCO / THE WAY OF SAINT FRANCIS

The Way of Saint Francis is a route which joins together some of the most significant places in Saint Francis' life. Unlike the Via Francigena or the Via Romea Germanica, it's a new route for today's pilgrims and those who simply enjoy walking. The whole walk from La Verna to Rome is roughly 500km long. It's a demanding walk as it involves a lot of going up and down, although of course you can always just walk individual sections. If you're planning to do the whole walk, or a large section

of it, make sure to send off for your Pilgrim's Credential and get it stamped when you set off. This is what gives proof that you've done the walk. (For details see **www.viadifrancesco.it.**) The walk is slightly different to the other routes in this book because its arrival point, Assisi, is in the middle of the route. In this sense there are two routes, one which comes down from the Sanctuary of La Verna in Tuscany and the other which comes up from Rome in the region of Lazio. Both arrive in Assisi, although you could also start in La Verna and make your way down to Assisi, and then continue to Rome.

Assisi is one of the most important places in the Catholic world. It was where Saint Francis was born and where he is buried in the Basilica di San Francesco. It's famous all over the world as a place of pilgrimage and for the frescoes by Giotto which are in it. Saint Francis died in October 1226 and within two years of his death he was made a saint by Pope Gregory IX. Work on the basilica began, and the first stone was laid by Pope Gregory IX on 17 July 1228. The piece of land on which the basilica would be built had previously been used for hanging criminals. It was on a hill known as Colle d'Inferno, literally

Basicila of Saint Francis of Assisi.
alexandro900 / Adobe Stock

Hell Hill. After two years, the Basilica Inferiore was finished. The remains of Saint Francis were transferred here from their original burial place in the Chiesa di San Giorgio, now the Basilica of Saint Clare, and the location kept secret to protect him from being stolen. It all remained a mystery for years until Pope Pius VII gave permission for investigations to begin at the beginning of the nineteenth century. Six hundred years after Saint Francis had died, on 12 December 1818 his remains were found under the altar. You can now go pay homage to the tomb, which underwent extensive restoration and was reopened in 2011. It is one of the most important pilgrimage sites in the world.

The Basilica di San Francesco, which was declared a UNESCO World Heritage site in 2000, is two basilicas: the Basilica Inferiore and the Basilica Superiore. The whole complex is made from the pink stone which is found on Mount Subasio. It's an impressive sight, a basilica truly fit for a saint, and even more so when lit up at night. The Basilica Inferiore is the first basilica which was commissioned by Pope Gregory IX. This is why it's known as a papal basilica because it was commissioned by a pope. The Basilica Superiore was completed later and in 1253 it was consecrated by Pope Innocent IV. Giotto's famous cycle of frescoes known as the *The Legend of Saint Francis* is here in the Basilica

Superiore, twenty-eight images which tell the life of Saint Francis. Not only are they a wonderful narrative of Saint Francis' life, but they also helped to change the course of art and were a precursor to the Renaissance. Giotto left behind the decorative paintings of the Middle Ages and its use of precious materials and focused on realistic portrayals of man and nature. They showed both emotion and place. They really are an incredible sight to behold, also because of their intensity of the colour and the blue of the sky. If a trip to Saint Francis' tomb is the spiritual pilgrimage, these frescoes represent the artistic pilgrimage. You can also see the original Rule of Order in which Pope Honorius III confirms the foundation of the Franciscan Order. It is dated 29 November 1223 and is displayed in the apse of the Basilica Superiore.

Assisi itself is a beautiful medieval town on the slopes of Monte Subasio, although like any major destination it can get very busy and you'll find souvenirs everywhere. While you're here, go visit the Sanctuary of the Eremo delle Carceri, the hermitage 4km out of Assisi up on Mount Subasio in the middle of an ancient holm oak forest. This is where Saint Francis and his monks went for periods of time to pray in silence. Carceri comes from the Latin *carcer*. Today, *carcere* in Italian actually means prison, but at the time of Saint Francis and his followers it was used to refer to those who followed isolated lives, alone, dedicated to prayer.[1] You can also see the Cave of Saint Francis where he slept on the rock. The Basilica di Santa Maria degli Angeli is in the valley at the foot of Assisi. This is where Saint Francis died in the small church of Porziuncola, which is now part of the Bascilica, and at the time was an infirmary where Saint Francis was cared for. The city also has a rich Roman past from the days when it was known as Assisium. You'll find the Temple of Minerva in Piazza del Comune. It's part of the Santa Maria sopra Minverva church. Underneath the square is the Roman Forum, centre of the political life and two Roman Domus or villas, Domus del Larium and Domus del Properzio. The Roman Forum was the centre of life in Roman times. It's been suggested that the Domus del Properzio belonged to the Roman poet Propertius because of poetry found on the walls.

La Verna to Assisi

The northern stretch of the walk is just under 200km long and ranges from challenging to easy, and there are two routes on the official website with slight differences. It starts at the Sanctuary of La Verna in the Casentino Forest National Park, where Saint Francis received the stigmata in 1224, two years before his death. It's an incredible place up on the cliff of Monte Penna with its sheer cliff face,

Santuario di La Verna. pergo70 / Adobe Stock

covered by a forest of beech and fir trees, almost removed from the rest of the world. This is the same cliff that Dante describes in his *Paradiso Canto XI*. Spend a day here to get a feel for the place and to fully appreciate its atmosphere, although bear in mind that this is one of the most important pilgrimage destinations in Italy and you certainly won't be alone. Visit the Cappella di Santa Maria degli Angeli, which was the first church built by Saint Francis up here in 1216 and is the place where Saint Francis worshipped. The Chapel of the Stigmata was built next door in 1263 on the exact place where Saint Francis received the stigmata. You can also see the stone slab which was his bed. Also go see the rock known as the Sasso Spicco, a huge cleft in the rock where the rock literally hangs over. It's where Saint Francis used to pray.

You can easily spend several hours and more just visiting the various monuments and taking in the atmosphere. To make sure that you're not rushing, you could stay in the village of Chiusi della Verna just below the cliff upon which La Verna stands, but make sure you book well in advance. The Via Romea Germanica also passes through the town and it's also home to the Sasso di Adamo (the Rock of Adam), a huge rock. It's said to be the rock which inspired the one Michelangelo painted in his *Creation of Adam* in the Sistine Chapel in Rome. The first part of the walk is wonderful

as you're walking through the Casentino Forests, just as Saint Francis would have done, and it really gives you a chance to experience the nature with which he felt so connected.

The walk takes you down to Assisi through the Valtiberiana, the Upper Tiber valley in the province of Arezzo in eastern Tuscany through which the River Tiber flows on its way to Rome. Pieve Santo Stefano is the first village you come across, along with various hermitages associated with the life of Saint Francis. The Eremo Cerbaiolo up on its rock is now empty, while the Eremo di Montecasale has a community of Cappuccino monks who offer food and lodging to pilgrims. Just outside Città di Castello is the Eremo di Buonriposo. *Buon riposo* means good rest, and this is where Saint Francis often rested.[2] Sansepulcro is where Piero della Francesca, one of the great painters of the Renaissance, was born, and then you're in Umbria. Citerna, known as the gate of Umbria, is one of the most beautiful *borghi* in Italy, and where Saint Francis performed two miracles. The next stages include Città di Castello, Pietralunga and Gubbio. Città di Castello is named after the city's castle. It's known for its fourteenth century tower known as the Torre Civica and its cathedral, the Cattedrale di Santi Florido e Amanzio, which was an important stop for pilgrims. Pietralunga is where you'll find the church Pieve de'

Saddi, a religious hostel for pilgrims and walkers. Gubbio merits a day or a stay. It was originally founded by the Umbri people, then home to the Etruscans and the Romans. In 552 it was invaded by the Goths and destroyed. The Byzantines then arrived, followed by the Longobards. During the Renaissance it was a thriving town which was famous for the production of majolica tiles, and it's still famous for its ceramics today. Palazzo Spadalonga was the home of the Spadalonga family, who offered Saint Francis his robe after he left Assisi and all his worldly possessions behind in 1206.

The last stretch of the Via di Francesca from Valfabricca to Assisi gives you the option of a detour to Perugia, Umbria's capital. Whatever you decide, Perugia is worth visiting for its wealth of artistic and historical treasures. When you get to Assisi, you'll go into the city through the medieval city gate, the Porta San Giacomo. This is where pilgrims left the city on their way to Santiago di Compostela, and thus the two routes are linked together, the Santiago di Compostela medieval pilgrimage, and the Via di San Francesco modern pilgrimage. Your destination is the Basilica di San Francesco and the tomb of Saint Francis. It's an emotional moment, whether you believe or not. Christianity is linked with the history and people of this beautiful land through the life of this much-loved saint.

Rome to Assisi

The route from Rome to Assisi is basically the route that Saint Francis took back to Assisi after he had been to Rome to see the Pope. Saint Francis went to Rome in 1210 because he wanted to ask Pope Innocent III permission to set up his brotherhood. The Pope said yes, and so he went back to Assisi and founded his order. The walk is roughly 300km long and like the northern route, there there are several variations which are all detailed on the official website. It starts at Saint Peter's Basilica in Rome and goes into the Valle Santa or holy valley. Rieti is the main town here. It was the ancient capital of what was once the area of the Sabines, an ancient Italic people who lived during the first millennium BC between Umbria, Lazio and Abruzzo until they were absorbed into the Roman Empire. It was considered the geographical centre of Italy by the Roman writer Marcus Terentius Varro. While you're here visit underground Rieti, where you'll find the old salt path, the Via Salaria. It was originally used by the Sabines and then by the Romans and linked Rome with Porto d'Ascoli on the Adriatic Sea. The town is famous for its four Franciscan sanctuaries: Santuario di Grecco, Santuario di Fonte Colombo, Santuario Santa Maria della Foresta and the Santuario di Poggio di Bustone.

The walk continues into Umbria, which brings the beautiful village of Spoleto where one of the only

Rocca Albornoziana, Spoleto. bbsferrari / Adobe Stock

surviving letters of Saint Francis is kept in the cathedral. Just before Spoleto is the Hermitage of Monteluco that Saint Francis is said to have founded, surrounded by its wood known as the Holy Wood. Spoleto is famous for its castle, the Rocca Albornoziana. Pope Innocent VI commissioned the castle, but he was in Avignon which was the papal seat at the time. So he sent Cardinal Albornoz, and hence the castle bears his name. From Spoleto as far as Assisi you'll go through the beautiful Umbrian countryside and places such as Poreta, Trevi, and Foligno. This area is known

for its olive oil, as you'll guess from the olive trees you'll see along the way, so do make time to stop and try it. Olive oil tasting is rather like wine tasting, only instead of wine you're given olive oil on bread. It really is an experience and makes you aware of how much taste and different tastes olive oil can have. The last section from Foligno to Assisi is just over 12km long and marked as easy, and if you only want to do a part of the walk, you could do this. It takes you through the village of Spello, listed as one of the most beautiful *borghi* or villages in Italy. It's halfway and the perfect place to stop for lunch. Spello has the best-preserved Roman city walls in Italy, and the city gates known as Porta Venere are a spectacular sight. If you have time, the Villa of Mosaics here is a Roman villa with a mosaic floor of beautiful geometric designs, animals, figures and scenes from life. When you arrive in Assisi, you'll go past the Basilica of Santa Chiara, dedicated to Saint Clare of Assisi. From Assisi, the walk then goes on to La Verna, should you wish, or you can choose sections of the walk as you please.

Eat

Assisi
Trattoria degli Umbri
This family-run restaurant specialises in local dishes in the town centre. It also has tables outside, perfect for summer dining and soaking up the atmosphere in the town.

Piazza del Comune, 40

Trattoria Pallotta
Trattoria Pallotta is in the Piazza del Comune under the arch of Volta Pinta. The arch has sixteenth century frescoes painted by Raffaellino del Colle and inspired by Roman remains found at the time. Go for typical Umbran food: home-made *pappardelle*, *strangozzi* with wild mushrooms, rabbit, pigeon, *torta al testo* and more.

Piazza del Comune, 3
www.trattoriapallotta.it

Chiusi della Verna
Locanda Il Sassone
Go for the *tortello alla lastra*, the local dish, a kind of sealed *piadina* filled with potatoes in tomato sauce and local home cooking. The restaurant is in Giampereta, just outside Chiusi della Verna.

Località Gimapereta, 23

Gubbio
La Cresciamia
Good value street food which specialises in the local bread *crescia* with all types of fillings. Also try the *brustengo*, a fried bread from Gubbio and the boards of cured meats known as *taglieri*.

Via Camillo Benso di Cavour, 23
www.lacresciamia.it

Spello
Osteria de Dadà
Restaurant in the centre of Spello which serves local food including antipasti to share, pasta and meat dishes.

Via Camillo Benso Conte di Cavour, 47

Spoleto
Taverna dei Duchi
Central restaurant which specialises in dishes from the area and the use of local produce such as truffle, Chianina meat, homemade pasta and cured meats from the Valnerina.

Via Aurelio Saffi, 1
www.tavernadeiduchi.it

Stay

Assisi

Casa Madonna della Pace

Stay with the nuns of the Franciscan Alcarine Sisters in the centre of Assisi in simple, welcoming accommodation in single, double, triple or quadruple rooms. They are also available to take groups of guests to the Franciscan sanctuaries in the area.

Via Bernardo da Quintavalle, 16 www.

Monastero San Giuseppe

The Benedictine nuns here offer accommodation in their guest house for families and individuals, either on a room only basis or with half board or full board lodging.

Via Sant'Appolinare, 1
www.msangiuseppe.it

Gubbio

Monastery of San Francesco

The monastery offers simple accommodation in shared rooms. Please note that you must bring your own sheet or sleeping bag.

Piazza 40 Martiri, 2
www.accoglienzasanfrancesco.it

Chiusi della Verna

Pastor Angelicus Casa per Ferie

Guest house run by the Franciscan Nuns of Saint Elizabeth at the foot of the Sanctuary of La Verna, right across from the path which leads up there.

They offer single rooms and rooms for 2/3/4/5 people. Accommodation is room only, half board or full board.

Viale San Francesco, 20
www.pastorangelicuslaverna.it

Letizia Albergo Ristorante

Charming hotel surrounded by the woods of the Casentino with owners who are always willing to offer suggestions for local walks. The restaurant offers local Tuscan dishes including freshly made pasta.

Via Roma, 26
www.albergo-letizia.it

Pieve di Saddi, Pietralunga

Stay at the parish hostel. To reserve a room, write to pievedesaddi@gmail.com

Località Pieve di Saddi, Pietralunga

Spello

Monastero Agostiniano Santa Maria Maddalena

Single, double and twin rooms at the guest house of the Agostinian nuns.

Via Camillo Benso di Cavour, 1
www.agostinianespello.it

Spoleto

Casa Religiosa di Ospitalità Nazareno

Stay with the Nuns of the Holy Family of Spoleto inside the city walls.

www.casanazareno.it

A Tale of Two Sisters: Saint Clare and Saint Agnes of Assisi

Saint Clare lived at the same time as Saint Francis and was also from a noble family, just like Saint Francis and Saint Benedict, who had lived 700 years earlier. Chiara Offredoccuio (Chiara is Clare in Italian) was born in Assisi on 16 July 1194. Her sister Catherine, afterwards known as Agnes, was born in 1197 or 1198. As a girl Clare already showed a desire to follow God, and when she was 18, she left home and went to join Saint Francis against her father's wishes. He wanted her to go back home but Clare refused and remained at the convent. Saint Francis sent her to the convent of the Benedictine nuns of San Paolo of San Paolo near Bastia Umbra and after several weeks to the monastery at Sant'Angelo in Panzo, where she was joined by her sister. When Clare was twenty-two, Saint Francis took Clare and Agnes to the church of San Damiano just outside the centre of Assisi and a convent was founded. The order was known as the Poor Ladies and Clare was made abbess. They were joined by their mother Ortolana, who had always been a religious woman, after their father died. Agnes later left the convent and went off to establish her own abbey in 1221 in Monticelli, near Florence. The nuns lived according to the vows of poverty,

Statue of Saint Clare, Assisi. ArTo / Adobe Stock

chastity, obedience and enclosure which means that they led cloistered lives and never left their convents, except for in special circumstances. When Saint Francis was ill and dying, he went to the convent at San Damiano and Saint Clare looked after him until his death. It was here that he wrote his *Canticle of the Creatures*. Clare died on 11 August 1253, while her sister Agnes died on 16 November of the same year. Two years later she was declared a saint by Pope Alexander IV, while Agnes was made a saint in 1753.

Maps, Links and Useful Information

Umbria
www.umbriatourism.it is the official website. It also has details of guided visits, events and where to stay.

Tuscany
www.visittuscany.com is the official website for Tuscany.

Lazio
www.visitlazio.com is the official Lazio website.

Via di Francesco
www.viadifrancesco.it is the official site with maps, itineraries and useful downloads about how to get your Pilgrim's Credential. They also have links to the official GPX if you're planning to walk using a navigator. Do read the information about getting to La Verna. If you go by car, you'll have to leave your car in nearby Chiusi della Verna and let the municipal police know. www.francescosways.com has a lot of useful information regarding routes and accommodation. They also organise tours in groups which cover both the walk and other walks within the area.

Casentino National Park
www.parcoforestecasentinesi.it is the official website with information and maps for paths and hiking trails. They also have a useful section 'Ten Rules of Safe Hiking'. Also see www.casentino.it for information about the area of the park in Tuscany, and www.visittuscany.com/attractions/foreste-casentinesi-national-park

Assisi
www.visit-assisi.it is the official website for Assisi and also has plenty of information about local events, traditions and where to stay and hotels.

Gubbio
www.old.comune.gubbio.pg.it is the local municipality website for tourism in Gubbio.

Perugia
www.turismo.comune.perugia.it is the local municipality website for tourism in Perugia.

Sanctuary of La Verna
www.laverna.it is the Sanctuary of La Verna's official website

Spoleto
www.comune.spoleto.pg.it is the local municipality website for tourism in Spoleto.

When to go
Bear in mind that in summer it can be very hot, so you're far better planning your walk for spring or autumn. Avoid winter as there may be snow.

While You're Here

- Go see the hermitage and monastery of Camaldoli in the area of the Casentino National Park, known as the forest of Camaldoli. It was founded a thousand years ago by Saint Romauld and is still home to the community of Benedictine monks who live there. They also have a foresteria or guest house which is open to those who wish to share in the spiritual life of the monastery and to those who are simply looking for accommodation. Just like when you visit the Sanctuary of La Verna, there is something about the mix of nature and religion which is so very powerful. **www.camaldoli.it**

- Visit the Regional Park of Monte Subasio, the mountain which the ancient Umbri people believed to be sacred. The main tourist attraction of course is Assisi, but it also includes the beautiful walled towns of Spello and Nocera Umbra, both of which are on the list of the most beautiful *borghi* or villages of Italy. For intineraries and walks, see **www.montesubasio.it**

- The Regional Park of Lake Trasimeno was historically known as the Lake of Perugia, which

Going up Mount Subasio along the Saint Francis Way. Andrea Vismara / Adobe Stock

Lake Trasimeno. GMfoto / Adobe Stock

gives an idea of how important it was. Head to Castiglione del Lago where Leonardo da Vinci and Niccolò Machiavelli both stayed. **www.parks.it/parco.trasimeno** has three itineraries for walks around the lake: around the island, historical itinerary and natural itinerary. They're a great way to explore this beautiful natural environment.

- Visit the Tiber Regional Park and walk along this famous river which leads to Rome. Todi and Orvieto are the main towns inside the park. They both have Etruscan origins, and treasures which include the Piazza del Popolo in Todi and the thirteenth century cathedral Duomo di Santa Maria Assunta in Cielo in Orvieto. Between Orvieto and Todi are the Forello Gorges, which wind their way through the landscape. The caves of Pozzi della Piana in Roccaccia near the village of Titignano are well worth a visit to see the stalagtites and stalagmites. The Eremo della Pasquarella is an eleventh century hermitage 13km out of Todi on the SS 448 in the hamlet of Acqualoreto. It's said to have been founded by Saint Romuald. Also take a walk along Lake Cobara and visit the village of Cobara with its castle and try Lago di Cobara DOC, the local wine. See www.umbriatourism.it/en/-/the-tiber-river-park

- Visit the town of Rieti with its thirteenth century town walls, city gates and underground salt path which dates to the time of the Sabines, the ancient population who lived here. Also visit the Franciscan monasteries, sanctuaries and villages in the Valle Santa. One of the most beautiful is Castel di Tora on Lake Turano. See www.visitrieti.com

CAMMINO DI SAN BENEDETTO / THE WAY OF SAINT BENEDICT

The Camino di San Benedetto, or Way of Saint Benedict as it's known in English, takes you through the heart of Umbria into Lazio as far as the border with Campania. It brings together three of the most important places of Saint Benedict's life: Norcia in the province of Perugia in Umbria; Subiaco, which comes under the Metropolitan City of Rome and is up in the mountains; and the Abbey of Montecassino in the province of Frosinone in Lazio. It's 300km long and there are sixteen stages. If you're planning to do the whole walk, you

Piazza di San Benedetto in Norcia. mikiphoto / Adobe Stock

can do it in sixteen days, although as always, don't rush if you don't feel up to it. It's far better to take longer but reach your destination. For many, it is a pilgrimage to pay their respects at the tomb of Saint Benedict in Montecassino. For others, it may be a way of discovering areas of Italy which you might not normally visit. It's certainly a way in to understanding a religious faith and its history, and the places and people who were involved.

Places tell so many stories. The beauty of this walk is that it takes you back far into a past before the Middle Ages, to a time of the Romans, when Christianity was still relatively young. Emperor Constantine was the first Roman emperor to convert to Christianity in 312 AD at the end of a period known as the Great Persecution, when Christians in Rome suffered terrible persecutions. When Emperor Constantine issued the Edict of Milan in February 313 and declared his conversion, he effectively gave permission for the Christians to exist. Christians were now allowed to worship freely, and they no longer had to do so secretly in the privacy of their homes. Paganism continued and was still allowed. Constantine kept the title of Pontifex Maximus, the title of Supreme High Priest. Emperor Gratian was the first to abandon the title when he became emperor in 367, and in 380 Emperor Theodosius proclaimed Christianity as the official religion of the state. Benedict was born just over a hundred years later in 480, and just four years after the Fall of the Roman Empire in 376. It was a time of political chaos, various epidemics, and there was a high level of poverty. Whereas the Roman Empire had unified Italy, when it fell, Italy was divided again. It would not be unified again until the Unification of Italy took place in 1861.

After the fall of the Roman Empire, foreign invaders arrived, and city states were formed. It wasn't until the eleventh century that a sense of stability started to return. This new stability was accompanied by growth in population and economy, and it was no coincidence that this was a time when pilgrimages became most popular. Europe became a safer place, and as a result it was safer to set off on pilgrimages, give or take various wars and invasions.

Norcia

The walk begins in the town of Norcia, the town where Saint Benedict was born, an ancient town originally populated by the Sabines in the Monti Sibillini national park. It's a beautiful position, up at an altitude of 600m on the mountain plain of Santa Scolastica, which was named after Benedict's sister. At the time when Saint Benedict was born, Norcia was already widely christianised. Benedict and Scolastica were born into a Christian family of Roman nobles, while there were plenty of hermits living Christian lives of devotion in the mountains and caves.[3]

There's a lot to see in Norcia as you would expect, so allow yourself a day to enjoy it before you do any walking. The main square is the Piazza San Benedetto, with its statue dedicated to Saint Benedict, the patron saint of Europe. It's also where you'll find some of Norcia's most important buildings. The Basilica di San Benedetto is the cathedral dedicated to Saint Benedict that was built on the site of the house Benedict grew up in with his sister Scolastica. It was built from the end of the thirteenth century onwards but has suffered damage from various earthquakes over the years. The most recent earthquake was in October 2016, two months after the earthquakes in Amatrice, Accumoli and Arquata del Trento. Many of Norcia's buildings were damaged, including the basilica. The bell tower of the basilica totally collapsed and the basilica suffered such damage that only the facade was left standing. This facade was held up for seven years until July 2023 when it was finally revealed again. It stands magnificently despite all it has endured, with its rose window and the statues of the four Evangelists, the saints Matthew, Mark, Luke and John. The Chiesa di Santa Maria Argentea and the thirteenth century Palazzo Communale are also here. Also visit the Complesso di Francesco, which has a rose window above the door. Norcia is famous for its rich culinary traditions, so do try and get a meal in while you're here, and take a look inside the town's delicatessens. Try both the *prosciutto di Norcia* and the local *salami di Norcia*.

As with any walk, make sure you check details regarding the Pilgrim's Credential before you travel, as you will be asked to show your Credential for certain accommodation. If you're planning to do the whole of the walk, you present this document on your arrival in Montecassino where you'll be given what's known as the Testimonium, proof that you've done the pilgrimage. Make sure that you ask for it to be stamped along the way. See www.camminodibenedetto.it for information.

Highlights of the walk include the village of Cascia, home of Saint Rita. Saint Rita lived here in the hamlet of Roccaporena in the home in which she was born, and later in her marital home before she became a nun after her husband was killed. She's now in the twentieth century basilica in the Capella di Santa Rita. Monteleone di Spoleto is the next stage of the walk, listed as one of Italy's most beautiful *borghi*. It's most famous for its sixth century Etruscan chariot. The chariot is now housed in the Metropolitan Museum of New York, although you can see a copy of it at the church and convent of Saint Francis, known as the Complesso Monumental di San Francesco. Rieti in Lazio is where the Cammino di San Benedetto crosses over with the Via di Francesco before it goes on to Assisi. The magnificent Castello di Rocca Sinibalda here was originally built in 1080. It underwent extensive renovation during the Renaissance and has impressive frescoes which date from this period. The walk then continues into the regional park of the Monti Lucretelli via the villages of Orvinio and Pozzaglia Sabino and the abandoned Abbazia di Santa Maria del Piano, which dates from the ninth century.

Then it's on to Subiaco, the second main stop on our route, where Saint Benedict went off to the mountains when he left Rome in the days when he was a student there.

Subiaco

Subiaco is in the Valle d'Aniene in the Regional Park of the Simbruini Mountains. It's the main town here, medieval and surrounded by its city walls. It's distinctive because of the Rocca Abbaziale di Subiaco, the fortified abbey at the top of the hill on which the town is situated. The Rocca Abbaziale was built at the end of the eleventh century by Pope John V who was the abbot of the Monastery of Saint Scholastic at the time. In this way the town was brought under the rule of the monastery. It's also known as the Rocca di Borgia, after the famous Borgia family. Rodrigo Borgia came here as governor in 1472. He was the

Sacro Specro, Subiaco. Adobe Stock

father of Lucrezia Borgia, who was born in Subiaco in 1480, and quite possibly in the Rocca Abbaziale.

Benedict set up a total of twelve monasteries in this valley, of which two remain. The most important for the Catholic Church is the Monastery of Saint Benedict, also known as the Sanctuary of the Sacro Speco or the holy cave, where so many come to worship from all over the world. It's a spectacular sight, this medieval monastery built into the side of Mount Taleo on the site of the Sacro Speco, the cave in which Benedict lived for three years. Its religious and historical impact is massive. Benedict came here at the beginning of the sixth century, lived in the cave for three years and then went back out into the world and changed the face of European monasticism. The implications of this were widespread throughout Western Europe. It's an impressive sight, not just for its physical presence but for all that it means.

The monastery was built at the end of the eleventh century on the site of the holy cave where Benedict lived. There are two churches, the

Subiaco. Freesurf / Adobe Stock

lower church and the upper church, which was built later above the lower church. Inside both churches there are various chapels and caves, all decorated with frescoes of the life of Saint Benedict and stories from the Bible. You can also visit the original Sacro Speco. Benedict lived in this cave for three years left for Montecassino to found the monastery there. Saint Francis made a pilgrimage here in 1223 and there's a portrait of him inside the Cappella di San Giorgio. It's said to be the oldest image of Saint Francis in existence. The Monastero di Santa Scolastica is also here which was founded in 520, its oldest part built on the remains of a villa belonging to the Emperor Nero.[4] It's the oldest Benedictine monastery in the world. It was originally called the Monastero di San Silvestro and wasn't known as the Monastero of Santa Scolastica until the fourteenth century. It's survived the Saracens, earthquakes and the bombings of the Second World War.

Subiaco is also famous because it was the home of the first printing press in Italy. The Subiaco Press was set up by two German monks, Arnold Pannartz and Konrad Sweynheim, in 1464.

Montecassino

In 529 Benedict left Subiaco and went to Montecassino to set up what would be remembered as the first Benedictine monastery founded according to the Benedictine Rule. The walk has six stages and takes you through the Regional Park of the Simbruini Mountains into the area known as the Ciociaria, in the province of Frosinone. Ciociaria comes from the word *ciocia*, which describes the type of shoe which was worn by the people in the mountains here. It had a flat sole with a pointed toe that went upwards and was strapped to the leg by laces.

Towns and villages here include Trevi nel Lazio, high up in the middle of the Monti Cantari, and Collepardo. Collepardo is in the Monti Ernici. Visit its thirteenth century Certosa di Trisulti and its Abbey of Casamari, the Benedictine monastery founded in the eleventh century. You'll also pass through Arpino and Roccasecca. Arpino is where Cicero was born, at the time known as Arpinum. Like all sons of Roman nobles, he was sent to Rome for his studies. Roccasecca was the birthplace of Saint Thomas Aquinas. The whole stretch from Subiaco to Montecassino is around 125km and because of the differences in altitude is quite demanding, especially in certain stretches. Always make sure you check the itineraries on the official website before setting off.

Our walk finishes at the Abbey of Montecassino, where Benedict

Abbey of Montecassino. kenzo / Adobe Stock

set up his first community of monks under his Benedictine Rule up on the mountain of the same name. When Benedict got to Montecassino in 529, he saw that pagan cults were still rife here.[5] Benedict destroyed it all and built his monastery here instead. His monastery was the first monastery officially under the Benedictine Rule. His sister Saint Scholastic was responsible for the first order of Benedictine nuns here. During the Second World War the monastery found itself along the Gustav Line, the main line of defence which the Germans used in 1944. The Allies believed the Germans were stationed at the monastery and attacked. The Battle of Montecassino was one of the bloodiest battles of the Second World War, with Allied casualties of 55,000. The abbey was destroyed and reduced to rubble.[6] After the war, the abbey was rebuilt and consecrated by Pope Paul VI on 24 October 1964. The museum here holds various objects from monastery's past.

Eat

Norcia
La Taverna del Boscaiolo
Typical restaurant which has been serving local dishes using high quality local ingredients for the past fifty years.

Via Bandieri, 7
www.tavernadelboscaiolo.it

Hosteria Sienti 'n può
Typical restaurant along Norcia's main street. Go for local dishes including the black truffle from Norcia, roast porcini mushrooms, freshly made pasta and meat dishes such as tripe, lamb and local Norcia sausages. They also have a selection of local beers.

Corso Sertorio, 46
www.ristorantenorcia.it

Subiaco
Belvedere Ristorante
The restaurant is situated along the road which leads up to the monasteries and offers a good selection of local dishes including *bruschetta*, lamb, scamorza cheese and local sausage.

Via Monasteri, 33
www.belvederesubiaco.com

Ristorante da Checcina
Also along the road leading up to the monasteries, this family run trattoria has been serving local dishes for the past sixty years. They also serve pizzas.

Via Monasteri, 42
www.dacecchina.com

Montecassino
Cristian Cennamo – Pizze di Ricerche
Simple restaurant serving gourmet pizzas. It's said to be one of the best places to eat pizza in the area.

Via Gemma de Bosis, 11

Trattoria Vecchia Cassino – Da Maria
The emphasis here is on using produce from the area of the Ciociaria, including a starter which comes from the traditions of the Benedictine monks.

Piazza Garibaldi, 6
www.trattoriamaria.it

Stay
Norcia
Norcia Ospitalità Il Capisterum
Hostel run by a local cooperative which promotes tourism in the area. They offer rooms near the swimming pool and economy rooms. They also organise excursions into the Sibillini Mountains National Park.

Via dell'Ospedale,
www.norciaospitilita.it

Affittacamera Residenza Montedoro
Elegant and welcoming rooms in the centre of Norcia with a view of the Sibillini mountains.

Via Francia, 26
www.residenzamontedoro.it

Subiaco
Monastero di Santa Scolastica
Stay at the Monastery of Saint Scholastic in Subiaco at the heart of it all. Accommodation is offered on a bed and breakfast or half board basis. The nuns also organise visits to the monastery.

Piazzale Santa Scolastica
You can find details about how to book on www.ospitalitareligiosa.it

Palazzo Moraschi
Sleep at this eighteenth century palazzo just outside the historical centre of Subiaco. Alongside the rooms, they also have several apartments.

Viale della Repubblica, 75
www.palazzomoraschisubiaco.it

Belvedere B&B
On the way up to the monasteries, this charming B&B is run by the same owners as the Ristorante Belvedere, and has wonderful views over Subiaco.

Via Monasteri, 33
www.belvederesubiaco.com

Montecassino
Hotel Piazza Marconi
Hotel right in the centre of Cassino overlooking the main street.

Via Giuglielmo Marconi, 25
www.hotelpiazzamarconi.it

Monastero di Santa Maria della Rupe
Accommodation for pilgrims at the monastery by the Benedictine nuns. It offers room only, bed and breakfast, half board and full board.

Via Montecassino
Details can be found at
www.ospitalitareligiosa.it

Maps, Links and Useful Information

Umbria
www.umbriatourism.it is the official website. It also has details of guided visits, events and where to say. Also see www.umbriatourism.net and www.umbriatourism.org

Lazio
www.visitlazio.com is the official Lazio website.

Cammino di San Benedetto
www.camminodisanbenedetto.it is the official site with maps, itineraries, lists of places to stay, information about the Benedictine community and the life of Saint Benedict. It also includes information about how to get your Pilgrim's Credential. They have links to the official GPX if you're planning to walk using a navigator.

www.francescosways.com also have information about the Cammino di San Benedetto.

Sibililini Mountains National Park
www.sibillini.net is the official website with information and maps for paths and hiking trails. Also see www.sibilliniweb.it

Norcia
www.borghipubelliditalia.it and www.umbriatourism.it both have information about Norcia.

The National Park of the Sibillini Mountains:

The wild and beautiful Sibillini Mountains National Park stretches across both Le Marche and Umbria, and it's worth spending a few days here if you can. It's an area which during the Middle Ages was associated with sybils, fairies, demons and other legends. It takes its name, Sibillini, from the Sybil of the Appenines who once lived here. In Umbria it stretches across into the south-east of the province of Perugia. Norcia is an essential destination, as is the mountain plain of Castelluccio di Norcia at an altitude of roughly 1,350m. There are three plains up there, the Pian Grande and the Pian Piccolo, which are both in the province of Perugia, and the Pian Perduto (literally, the Lost Plain) which is in the province of Macerata in Marche. These plains come to life in a magnificent display of spring flowers between May and July, which includes poppies, daffodils, gentians and violets. The village of Castelluccio di Norcia is the perfect base to explore the local area and has breathtaking views of the surrounding mountains. Also visit Preci and the Lu Cugnuntu waterfalls, which you can walk up to from San Lazzaro in Valloncello, a hamlet of Preci.

The official website is www.sibillini.net

Preci. shalith / Adobe Stock

Castelluccio di Norcia. methanora / Adobe Stock

Subiaco
www.subiacoturismo.it
www.turismoroma.it
www.e-borghi.it
and www.visititaly.com all have
information.

Monastero di San Benedetto
www.monasterosanbenedettosubiaco.it
is the official website for the Monastery
of Saint Benedict.

Abbazzia di Montecassino
www.abbazziamontecassino.it is
the official website for the Abbey of
Montecassino

When to go
Do bear in mind that summer can be
very hot. Spring and autumn are better
periods for walking.

GETTING HERE AND GETTING AROUND

Umbria's airport is in Perugia, whereas
Rome is the obvious choice if you're
wanting to walk the sections in Lazio.
The main airport in Tuscany is Florence.
Rail links are generally good. The
nearest train station to Norcia is 40km
away in Spoleto, on the main Rome –
Ancona line. Assisi station is on the
Rome – Florence line and 3km outside
the town with a regular bus service into
town. Cassino is on the main Rome –
Naples train line. There is a direct coach
which links Subiaco with Rome.

6

TO ROME AND BEYOND

→ Via Francigena – Canterbury to Rome
  • Montefiascone to Rome

INTRODUCTION

All roads lead to Rome, as French theologist Alain de Lille wrote in 1175. Rome was always a popular destination for pilgrimages, although during the Middle Ages the most popular pilgrimage in Europe was to Santiago de Compostela to see the tomb of Saint James, and of course to the Holy Land. In 1300 however, year of the Jubilee, Pope Boniface VIII decided that it was no longer necessary to travel to the Holy Land. A pilgrimage to Rome would do just as well. Rome became the destination for many.[1]

We've seen how two of the three main routes that brought pilgrims across Europe to Rome came down through Italy. The Via Francigena came from Canterbury through France and Switzerland and followed the route of Sigeric. Sigeric recorded the route on his way back from Rome after he'd received the pallium from the Pope in 990. The Via Romea Germanica brought pilgrims down from Stade in the north of Germany. It was recorded by Albert of Stade when he went to Rome to see the Pope, this time to ask to change the order of his monastery. The Via Romea Strata brings together various *Vie Romei* (roads to Rome) and Roman roads in from the east of Europe into the north of Italy. It then goes down into Tuscany at Fucecchio, where it joins the Via Francigena.

Our pilgrims walked for miles and weeks and months. They came over the Alps, through the Alpine regions, saw world-famous mountains such as the Dolomites and the 4,000m summits of the Aosta Valley. They faced the elements, a few bandits along the way, some of them fell ill. They saw churches, towns, mountains, plains, rivers, witnessing it all as the landscape changed from north to south. They'd heard many different dialects alongside the beginnings of the Italian language as we know it today. Maybe they'd bought a few medieval souvenirs along the way.

Luciano Mortula - LGM / Adobe Stock

These were often badges or miniature reliquaries made by local artists.[2] Sometimes pilgrims took relics and various other precious items back home them with. Whether this was always legal or not is another question. There's also the issue of whether the object was what it was supposed to be.[3] In this last chapter, I'll look at one of the most popular stretches of Italy's pilgrimages, the Via Francigena from northern Lazio into Rome. I'll be treating this as one whole stretch, with the aim of getting your Testimonium of having walked the Via Francigena. Of course you can always split it up, walk sections, spend a few days sightseeing, go for a short walk and lunch. It really is up to you.

VIA FRANCIGENA

Tuscia

The last stage of the Via Francigena to Rome takes you through northern Lazio and what is now known as Tuscia. In ancient times it was called Etruria. It's where the Etrucans lived before they were eventually taken over by the Romans. Tuscia is the name that was given to the area after the Etrurians lost power, and particularly from the Middle Ages onwards. It

Civita di Bagnoregio. SimoneGiulioili / Adobe Stock

comes from the *Tusci* who lived there. It's also where we get Tuscany from as this too was also partially in Etruria. Tuscia covers the whole province of Viterbo and has wonderful medieval hilltop villages such as Civita di Bagnoregio, Caprarola, Vitorchiano, Calcata, Bomarzo, and Tarquinia, which is famous for its Etruscan necropolis. It's also famous for is food and wine, making it the perfect area to spend time in and do some walking before moving on to Rome.

From Montefiascone to Rome

The 45th and last stage of the Via Francigena starts in La Storta, although if you want to get your Via Francigena Testimonium, you'll need to show that you've walked at least 100km or at least from Viterbo, according to the official Via Romea Germanica website. In this case start in Montefiascone, which according to the official Via Francigena website is the one hundredth kilometre before the Tomb of Saint Peter. It's the seventh stage along Sigeric's itinerary, which he recorded in reverse from Rome to Canterbury.[4] Montefiascone is the 39th stage of the walk. The final stage of the walk from La Storta to Rome is the 45th so if you calculate a day for each stage, you're looking at a week's walking. As always, the best maps you can use are those on the Via Francigena app or on the official website **www.viafrancigena.org.**

These maps are always up to date and will give you information about anything you should know such as deviations in the route. They have a page within the website named 'criticalities of the walking path' where you can find all recent updates. Bear in mind that if you are planning to walk from Montefiascone to Rome, you'll be walking around 20-25km per day, which can mean six to seven hours walking. As always, if you're unsure, split it up further and take your time. The beauty of this walk is that it gives you the chance to see a part of Italy which you might not necessarily visit otherwise, and yet which has so much to offer the tourist. If you're thinking of walking sections of the walk, do the walk between Montefiascone and Viterbo. It's a mainly downhill route to begin with, with some upwards elevation later. It takes you along the hills and gives you wonderful views of the surrounding countryside, including the towns themselves. It's a great way to enjoy walking part of the Via Francigena, and you can always take the bus back to where you started from!

Montefiascone

Our walk begins in Montefiascone, near Lake Bolsena, up on the hill and with a wonderful view of the lake. The town is famous for its medieval fortress, the Rocca dei Papi (Fortress of the Popes), which was built by Pope Innocent III at the end of the thirteenth century.

Also visit the eleventh century Chiesa di San Flaviano, which you'll find along the Via Francigena just outside the town, and the Chiesa di Santa Margherita, the city's Duomo. It was built in 1674, is the second largest basilica in Italy and has seven chapels inside it. The town is best known for its Est! Est!! Est!!! wine that attracts wine-lovers from all over the world. It's a dry white wine that you can try in the various wine cellars or *cantine* around town. You'll also see it on the menus in the town's restaurants and bars. You might also want to take time to try the local dishes. Soups are popular such as *acquacotta*, made with

Montefiascone. e55evu / Adobe Stock

stale bread and chicory, and *zuppa di castagne,* which makes use of the chestnuts from the local mountains, the Monti Cimini.

Montefiascone to Viterbo

The next stage of the walk leaves Montefiascone from the fortress of the Rocca dei Papi and takes you to Viterbo. It takes you along part of the Via Cassia, an ancient Roman road. The Via Cassia passed through Etruria at Sutria and then Bolseno, the town on the lake of the same name. It was a military route built around the third and second centuries BC, and connected Rome with Florence. When you arrive in Viterbo, there's plenty to see. Viterbo is the capital of Tuscia and was known as the Città dei Papi (City of the Popes) because it was seat of the Holy See between 1257 and 1281. At that time, Rome had become increasingly hostile politically. Pope Alexander IV moved the papacy to Viterbo because it offered a safer place away from Rome. You can visit the Palazzo dei Papi where the popes lived in Piazza San Lorenzo. Also visit the Cattedrale di San Lorenzo, which was built on the site of the original late eighth century church, and the Colle del Duomo Museum, both also in Piazza San Lorenzo. Viterbo is also known for its historical centre and the beautifully preserved quarter of San Pellegrino, one of the largest medieval

Viterbo. Riccardo Spinella / Adobe Stock

quarters in Europe. Give yourself time to wander around and soak up the beauty of its atmosphere.

Viterbo to Vetralla

The next stage of the walk takes you as far as Vetralla, through various woods and the village of San Martino al Cimino. San Martino al Cimino is a hamlet of Viterbo about 7km out of the town of Viterbo. It's up on its hill at an altitude of 571m, near the bottom of Mount Fogliano near Lake Vico, where there's a nature reserve here if you want to go explore. The village is known for its Cistercian abbey that you'll find in the centre, and for its porcini mushrooms. Look out for them on the menu. You'll see them fried, served with tagliatelle, and roasted with potatoes. There's also a local soup with porcini mushrooms and potatoes. It also produces excellent oil. If you have time, also visit the Faggeta Vetusta del Monte Cimino. These ancient beech forests received UNESCO World Heritage Status in 2017.

Vetralla to Sutri

From Vetralla it's then on to Sutri, which is where the Via Cassia passed through on its way out of Rome. Sigeric mentions Sutri as his fourth stop on his way out of Rome. He calls it *Suteria,* which comes from its Etruscan name of *Suthrina. Suthrina* in its turn refers to Saturn, one of the gods that the Etruscans worshipped.[5] The town was called the 'Gate of Etruria' by the Roman historian Livius as it's here that the ancient region of Etruria begins, just over 50km outside Rome. Sutri is built on a small tuff hill. Tuff is the volcanic ash which formed hills in the area, and which were obviously attractive locations for Etruscan settlements. The town is best known for its first century Roman amphitheatre,

The Roman amphitheatre at Sutri.
anghifoto / Adobe Stock

which was dug out of the tuff and for its Etruscan necropolis, around sixty-four ancient rock tombs. During the Etruscan period it was a thriving commercial and agricultural centre, while during the Middle Ages it was an important passing place for merchants and pilgrims on their way to Rome.

Sutri to Campagnano di Roma

The walk leaves Sutri from the Roman amphitheatre and takes you onwards through two regional parks before you get to the town of Campagnano di Roma. The first is the Parco Naturale Regionale Valle del Treja, which you'll get to after passing a small hamlet known as Monterosi. If you fancy a coffee, then stop here. The next point of interest is the Cascate di Monte Gelato, the waterfalls which are inside the Valle del Treja park and is a lovely place to have a rest and a sandwich. The second regional park is the Parco Naturale Regionale di Veio. It's known for its Isola Farnese, a small hamlet which you'll pass on the next stage of the walk.

When you reach Campagnano di Roma, you are now in what's known as the *Città metropolitana di Roma Capitale* (the Metropolitan City of Rome Capital). In other words, you're nearly there. It's roughly about 33km to Rome now. The town has four churches which are of interest, and like Sutri was an important centre for trade and pilgrims on the way to Rome.

Cascate di Monte Gelato. puckillustrations / Adobe Stock

Campagnano di Roma to La Storta

The road from Campagnano di Roma is when you start to spot Rome in the distance.

There are two points of interest on the route, the Santuario della Madonna del Sorbo and Isola Farnese. The Santuario della Madonna del Sorbo is up on a cliff along the Valle del Sorbo in the Parco di Veio. It began life as a tenth century castle and was later transformed into a monastery for Carmelite monks. The walk continues to the village of Formello, where you could stop for lunch. Take a look inside Palazzo Chigi, which is also a hostel, should you wish to stay the night. After Formello, you continue walking until you reach the second point of interest, the hamlet of Isola Farnese, which is also in the Parco del Veio. It's situated on a volcanic cliff and takes the name of *isola* or island because at one time it was surround by streams and a moat. The presence of a village dates from the Middle Ages when it was known as *Castrum Insulae,* or the island castle, although there are also Roman ruins. When you arrive in La Storta, you've reached the last stage of the Via Francigena. You are now only 19km from Rome.

Areial view of Isola Farnese, surrounded by its moat. Claudio Quacquarelli / Adobe Stock

La Storta to Saint Peter's Basilica, Rome

The first stretch as you leave La Storta isn't the most picturesque as you are getting towards the city and you'll be walking along a busy road. After this, you'll go into the Riserva Naturale dell'Insugherato, a nature reserve with various ruins of Roman villas and tombs, and an Etruscan settlement that

was discovered in 1999. It provides a moment of calm and opportunity for reflection before you start to enter the city of Rome. After this, it's back out into the traffic and along the Via Trionfale until you reach the Parco di Monte Mario, a park up on the hill known as Monte Mario just outside Rome, which has a wonderful view of Rome. It's also known as Monte della

Gioia or *Mons Gaudii* and it's easy to see why. There in front of you is the city of Rome, with the Dome of Saint Peter's Basilica. It's a view that so many pilgrims have enjoyed as they neared Rome, and which has inspired poets, writers and artists over the years. The Zodiaco terrace is the best spot near the city's Osservatorio Astronomico at the top of the hill. It really is a sight for sore eyes (and legs)!

After enjoying the view from Monte Mario, it's then back down into the city and traffic and to your final destination of Saint Peter's Basilica.

THE ARRIVAL IN ROME

The arrival in Rome was, and is, always a big event. Rome was known as the City of the Apostles because this was where Saint Peter and Saint Paul had lived and where they were buried. The most precious Christian relics are those that relate to Christ or the Apostles, and here are the tombs of Saint Peter and Saint Paul. If you went to see the relics of the Apostles, this was a way to get nearer to God, and by going to Rome this is exactly what you were doing.[6]

The site where Saint Paul was buried is under the Basilica di San Paolo Fuori le Mura (Basilica of St Paul Outside the Walls). It's one of Rome's four main basilicas and the city's second-largest church. Saint Paul's tomb is underneath the main altar. He was buried here after he was decapitated in 67. Saint Peter was the first bishop of Rome and was crucified at the Circus of Nero on the orders of Emperor Nero. He's buried on

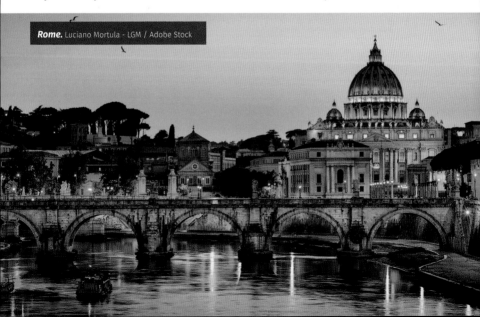

Rome. Luciano Mortula - LGM / Adobe Stock

Vatican Hill, under the Basilica di San Pietro (Saint Peter's Basilica). Whether you were a pilgrim of the past or a pilgrim of today, a visit to the tombs of Saint Peter and Saint Paul is one of the most deeply moving experiences you can imagine.

Of course, once you got to Rome, you then had to go back, undertake the same journey, run the same risks, and face the same hardships. Yet so many did it. They went to Rome and then went back home again. That is how powerful faith can be. Nowadays you can obviously get on a plane or train or drive, yet there is something so special about walking into Rome. It's not only the act of pilgrimage or the opportunity to enjoy a slower form of tourism. It's also the chance to forge a deep connection with personal faith and/or the past.

Rome is literally packed with history. Wherever you go, whichever street corner you turn, there's something to see. You turn a corner and walk into a square and there is the Pantheon in front of you. It's over 2,000 years old and was originally a pagan temple. Then in 608 Pope Boniface IV ordered the remains of Christian martyrs to be moved there and its status as a pagan temple was changed to that of a Christian church. Walk down another street and there are the Spanish Steps, which lead up from the Piazza di Spagna to the Chiesa della Trinità dei Monti at the top. The Roman Forum is incredible, and still very much a presence in Rome. It was the centre of public life, where laws were made, people worshipped at the temples and went shopping at the markets. The Colosseum was built between 70 and 72 according to the wishes of the Emperor Vespasian and is a must-see while you're here. Of course, the list is endless. Do try and give yourself at least a few days to enjoy the city when you arrive.

What you will also notice about Rome are its people. If you ask for directions, you feel like they would take you there. They chatter and gesticulate to each other using Roman expressions and Roman words, and all the time you're wishing you could just stay longer. The first century Roman poet Marcus Annaeus Lucanus called Rome *Roma caput mundi*, Rome, master of the world. The Roman Empire is long gone, but the history of its glory remains. It is all around you. When you walk around Rome, you are walking in the traces of those who helped shape the history of western civilisation. It's an impressive thought. Speaking of which, if you've had enough of walking by this time, get on a tourist bus. It's a great way to see the main sights and an enjoyable way to spend an afternoon.

This is where our journey ends for now, at the Basilicas of Saint Peter and Saint Paul. At the end you'll find a taster of what is still to come, once you go past Rome and enter the lands of the south.

Saint Peter's Basilica

Saint Peter was Jesus' chief apostle and the apostle to whom Jesus first appeared after the Resurrection. Jesus called him 'Petros' or 'rock' and for Catholics he is the rock upon whom the church is built. The church in which he is buried is, to give it its full title, the Papal Basilica of Saint Peter in the Vatican. It's a papal basilica because it was commissioned by a pope. Pope Nicholas V had the idea of building a new basilica as the old basilica, which had been commissioned by Emperor Constantine back in 326, was in a state of disrepair. The old basilica was destroyed, and the building of the new basilica started in 1506 when Pope Julius V laid the first stone and ended in 1626. The original architect was Bramante. He died in 1514, and a mere eight years after building had begun, it started to grind to a halt. Then in 1547 Michelangelo was commissioned as chief architect and things started to get moving again. He'd already painted the frescoes inside the Sistine Chapel. He now designed the dome but did not live to see it built. Pope Julius II commissioned Michelangelo to paint the frescoes on the ceiling of the Sistine Chapel in 1508. They were finished in 1512

and depict scenes from the Old Testament and are one of the greatest works of art that we have today. The chapel is full of frescoes by many important Renaissance artists, alongside

Saint Peter's Basilica, Rome.
Mapics / Adobe Stock

two other important frescoes by Michelangelo on the west wall of the chapel. The Sistine Chapel is the pope's chapel, and the seat of the Papal Conclave where the cardinals gather to elect a new pope. The basilica was eventually finished by Carlo Moderno and consecrated by Pope Urban VIII on 18 November 1626.

www.basilicasanpietro.va

Basilica of Saint Paul Outside the Walls

Emperor Constantine also commissioned the original Basilica of Saint Paul, which was consecrated by Pope Sylvester in 330. It's one of Rome's four papal basilicas. The other two are the Arcibasilica di San Giovanni in Laterano and the Basilica di Santa Maria Maggiore. It was extended after it was built in 330 towards the end of the fourth century and was Rome's largest basilica until Saint Peter's Basilica was consecrated in 1626. In 1823 it was destroyed by a terrible fire, and afterwards rebuilt. This was after an earthquake had already taken place back in 433. Celebrations took place for the jubilee in 2000, but nobody actually knew where Saint Paul was. Investigations then began and in 2006 a stone coffin with the markings *Paulo Apostolo Mart* (Saint Paul martyr) was found underneath the basilica. The remains in the coffin were confirmed as belonging to the time of Saint Paul by the Vatican in 2009. You can now see Saint Paul's coffin through a small window when you visit the basilica.

www.basilicasanpaolo.org

Basilica of Saint Paul Outside The Walls. Iván Moreno / Adobe Stock

LOCAL FOOD

One of the best ways to enjoy Rome, apart from all the sightseeing, is via its food. Pasta takes centre stage. You'll find *tonnarelli alla carbonara* and *tonnarelli cacio e pepe*. *Tonnarelli* is a type of spaghetti from Lazio. *Carbonara* is made with *guanciale*, egg yolks and *pecorino romano* cheese, whereas *cacio e pepe* is made with *pecorono romano* cheese and pepper. It all sounds very simple in theory but to make it well is an art form. *Tonnarelli alla gricia* is served with *guanciale*, *pecorino romano* and black pepper. *Bucatini all'amatriciana* is made using *bucatini*, a larger type of spaghetti with a hole running through the middle of it. The *amatriciana* sauce is like that of *gricia*, only with tomatoes added. Main courses include *coda alla vaccinara* (stewed oxtail) and *abbacchio scottadito* (grilled lamb chops). *Carciofi alla giudia* (fried artichokes) is a Jewish dish which originated in Rome's Jewish quarters in the sixteenth century. *Carciofi alla romana* are artichokes stewed with garlic, parsley and mint. You'll also find what's known as the *quinto quarto* or offal, which include *trippa alla romana* (Roman-style tripe). For breakfast try a *maritozzo*, a typical pastry filled with whipped cream.

Artichokes known as *carciofi alla giudia*. Rachael Martin

Eat

Montefiascone
Mamma Pappa
Typical restaurant in Montefiascone's historical centre that serves local cooking. Also try the desserts.

Largo del Plebiscito, 4

Viterbo
Trattoria L'Archetto
Situated in the historical centre of Viterbo with tables outside for *al fresco* eating, this charming trattoria specialises in seasonal local specialities.

Via Santo Cristoforo, 1

Il Gargolo
Also in the historical centre with tables outside in the square with a selection of local dishes.

Piazza della Morte, 15

Vetralla
Pinseria 06
The speciality is the Roman *pinsa*, a type of long, thick pizza, which is served with various toppings, and is always a popular favourite. The restaurant is in the historical centre and also has tables outside for summer dining.

Sutri
Il Localetto
Restaurant and pizzeria in the historical centre of Sutri, which specialises in local meat dishes.

Via Vittorio Veneto, 35
www.illocaletto.it

Campagnano di Roma
Osteria Pizzeria da Miccione
Home cooked traditional Roman dishes, including local pasta dishes and *carciofi alla giudia* (deep-fried artichoke). It's definitely one to add to your list.

Piazza Regina Elena, 23
www.

Rome
The trick in Rome is to stay away from the tourist areas and look out for the trattorias and osterias which you'll spot down the side streets. You could also try the following: Da Gino al Parlamento **www.ristorante.parlamento.it** and Osteria da Mario, also near the Quirinale (Piazza delle Copelle, 51)

Stay

Along the Via Francigena
The Via Francigena website has a complete list of accommodation at the official website www.viafrancigena.org. You'll find it under the section 'accommodation and facilities'. They also indicate which structures have the stamp for your Pilgrim's Credential. You will need these stamps to get your Testimonium. Note that some places also provide food. If you prefer to stay somewhere quiet as you near Rome, then consider staying in the area around the Isola Farnese.

Rome
Rome is vast and it all depends upon where you want to be. The viafrancigena.org website has a complete list of accommodation.

If you're planning to spend a few days in Rome, then base yourself slightly outside the centre. Testaccio is a good area in which to stay as you can then get a bus into the centre easily enough. It has various bed and breakfasts, typical trattorias and offers an insight into daily Roman life. If you do decide to stay in Testaccio, then try both Da Bucatino (www.dabucatino.it) and Lo Scopettaro (www.loscopettaro.com) for traditional Roman dishes.

Maps, Links and Useful Information

Lazio
www.lazioturismo.com
www.lazio.nascosto.it

Rome
www.romaturismo.it

Via Francigena
www.viafrancigena.org

Tuscia
www.tusciaturismo
www.promotuscia.it
www.tusciawelcome.it
www.visitarelatuscia.it

Viterbo
www.infoviterbo.it
www.visit.viterbo.it

While You're Here

- Visit the village of Calcata in the Valle del Treja. At one time Calcata was left abandoned, but then in the 1960s it was rediscovered by hippies and since then has maintained its popularity with creatives from nearby Rome to the point that it was once called a 'little Rome'. Spend time exploring the old town and visit the Valle del Treja around you.

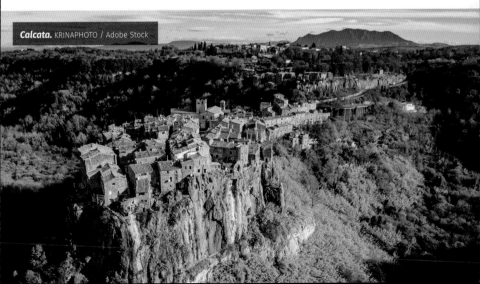

Calcata. KRINAPHOTO / Adobe Stock

Capodimonte, Lake Bolsena. FPWing

- Tarquinia was once the capital of Etruria and is famous for its Etruscan necropolis which dates from the seventh century BC. You can visit twenty-two tombs and see the incredible paintings that give you an insight into Etruscan life. Also visit the archaeological museum, the Museo Archeologico Nazionale di Tarquinia, in the fifteenth century Palazzo Vitelleschi. The town's medieval historical centre is a lovely place to explore with its various churches and palazzos. Tarquinia is right near the coast so spend time at the seaside at nearby Lido di Tarquinia. www.tarquiniaturismo.com
- Civita di Bagnoregio is known as the *città che muore*, the city that dies, because it was built on tuff, the volcanic ash that formed steep hills in the area. It's in a spectacular position in the Valle dei Calanchi, the Valley of the Badlands. It's a lovely place to explore, with characteristic stone houses and cobbled streets, shops, restaurants and bars and various medieval churches. Please note that you can only arrive in Civita di Bagnoregio via the suspended bridge that links it with Bagnoregio.
- Lake Bolsena is Europe's largest volcanic lake and known for the beauty of its villages, natural environment and walking opportunities. Capodimonte is one of its prettiest villages, and a great place for a leisurely lunch.

GETTING HERE AND GETTING AROUND

Rome is obviously the nearest airport, after which you can get the northern line train which goes to Viterbo. The province of Viterbo has a bus service which connects the various towns.

BEYOND ROME

Our journey ends in Rome. Beyond Rome lies the south of Italy, where the intense heat of the summers are accompanied by the sound of the cicadas. After Lazio, we move into Campania. Naples is the capital, with the Amalfi Coast and Cilento on the coasts beyond. The Sentiero degli Dei goes along the Amalfi Coast and offers stunning views of this much-loved Italian coastline. After this it's down into Basilicata and towns such as Matera, where the Cammino Materano ends, and then onwards to Calabria. The Appenines come right down to the bottom of the Italian peninsula and across into Sicily. They are rugged, wild and often remote. On the eastern coast of southern Italy, there is the small region of Molise and then Puglia, which forms the heel. The landscape is flatter here in Puglia. This is where the Vie delle Transumanze (Ways of the Transhumance) come, the old roads which were used to bring the animals from the mountains in Abruzzo down to Puglia for the winter months. These ways tell different stories of other places and people; stories to be kept for another day.

Olive grove, Puglia.
Massimo Santi / Adobe Stock

ENDNOTES

Introduction: Sentiero Italia
1 Basilicò and Furlanetto, *Va' Sentiero*, p. 19
2 Basilicò and Furlanetto, *Va' Sentiero*, p. 134

1. The Via Francigena and the Aosta Valley
1 Gorgoza, (2022), The 'Brides of Mont Blanc': Europe's earliest female mountaineers Available at https://english.elpais.com (first accessed 20 May 2023)
2 Biblioteca Renato Nicolini, (2020), *Alpinismo Rosa: la storia di Marie Paradis* Available at www.bibliotechediroma.it/opac/news/alpinismo-rosa-la-storia-di-marie-paradis/26254 (first accessed 20 May 2023)
3 Gorgoza, (2022), The 'Brides of Mont Blanc': Europe's earliest female mountaineers Available at https://english.elpais.com (first accessed 20 May 2023)
4 www.montebianco.com (first accessed 17 May 2023)
5 www.matterhornparadise.ch (first accessed 10 July 2023)
6 Bragg, M. (2021, 18 February), Medieval Pilgrimage (Audio podcast episode) In *In Our Time: Religion*, BBC Radio Four
7 www.vatican.va *The Use of the Pallium* (first accessed 1 June 2023)

8 www.bl.uk Collection items: Itinerary of Archbishop Sigeric (first accessed 1 June 2023)
9 www.digiliblt.uniupo.it, Iterarium Burdigalense (first accessed May 2023)

2. From Milan to Lake Como to Switzerland
1 Fondazione Politecnico di Milano, *I Cammini della Regina, percorsi transfrontalieri legati alla via Regina* [Video] www.regina.eu/ (first accessed 18 August 2023).
2 Fondazione Politecnico di Milano, *L'Antica Via Regina*, www.viaregina.eu/(first accessed 18 August 2023)
3 Birch, *Pilgrimage to Rome in the Middle Ages*, p. 50
4 *Le Vie del Viandante: Percorrre a piedi la storia, dal Lago di Como a San Bernardino, attraverso la Valle Mesolcina*, p. 9
5 Merisio, *Via Sett Via Spluga: da Thusis a Chiavenna: due percorsi, mille emozioni*, p. 120
6 Bracci, *Viaggio in Italia: a piedi in mountain-bike attraverso le Alpi - Via Spluga - e gli Appenini - da Bologna a Firenze*, p. 53
7 *Le Strade dello Spluga*, www.ecomuseovalledellospluga.it
8 Faggiani, *Le Meraviglie delle Alpi: Natura, Cultura, Cammini e Racconti* pp. 97-9

3. Emilia-Romagna
1   *La Via Emilia*, www.
    emiliaromagnatourism.it (first
    accessed 2 June 2023)
2   www.catholic.com *Albert of Stade*
    Available at https://www.catholic.
    com/encyclopedia/albert-of-
    stadefirst (first accessed 1 June 2023)
3   Bragg, M. (2021, 18 February),
    Medieval Pilgrimage (Audio podcast
    episode) In *In Our Time: Religion*,
    BBC Radio Four
4   *Romea Strata: un percorso di fede,
    storia e natura* (2020) www.repubblica.
    it (first accessed 28 September 2023)
5   www.viaromeagermanica.com
6   Russo, *L'Italia è un Sentiero*, p.114

4. Tuscany and the Way to Rome
1   *Il cibo dei pelligrini: cosa
    mangiavano lungo la Via
    Francigena?*, 1 February 2016, www.
    lacucinaitaliana.it (first accessed
    23 August 2023)
2   *Via Francigena*, Touring Club Italiano,
    p. 120
3   *La Fauna*, www.
    parcoforestecasentinesi.it (first
    accessed 24 September 2023)

5. Umbria and the Ways of the Saints
1   www.santuarioeremodellecarceri.org
    (first accessed 13 September 2023)
2   Ardito, La Via di Francesco, p. 47
3   Frignani, Simone, *Cammino di San
    Benedetto* in *Cammini Italia: I migliori
    itinerari*, edited by Ardito, p. 210

4   Frignani, Simone, *Cammino di
    San Benedetto* in *Cammini Italia:
    I migliori itinerari*, edited by Ardito,
    p. 215
5   Frignani, Simone, *Cammino di
    San Benedetto* in *Cammini Italia:
    I migliori itinerari*, edited by Ardito,
    p. 217
6   The National WWII Museum
    Orleans, (2021) *The Destruction of
    Monte Cassino*. Available at www.
    nationalww2museum.org/war/
    articles/destruction-of-monte-
    cassino-1944 (first accessed
    17 September 2023)

6. Rome and Beyond
1   Van Herwaarden, Jan, *Viaggi Romei
    dai Paesi Nordici*, in *Romei e Giubilei*,
    edited by d'Onofrio, pp. 101-102
2   Sorabella, Jean, *Pilgrimage in
    Medieval Europe*, (2000) Available at
    www.metmuseum.org (first accessed
    31 May 2023)
3   Van Herwaarden, Jan, *Viaggi Romei
    dai Paesi Nordici*, in *Romei e Giubilei*,
    edited by d'Onofrio, p. 104
4   *Montefiascone, città del 100° Km
    dalla Tomba di Pietro*, available at
    www.viafrancigena.org (first accessed
    27 September 2023)
5   Touring Club Italia, *Via Francigena*,
    p. 164
6   Drake Boehm, Barbara, *Relics and
    Reliquiaries in Medieval Christianity*,
    Available at www.metmuseum.org
    (first accessed 27 September 2023)

INDEX